RIVERS CHANGING

A Solo Canoeing Adventure

Gordon Galloway

DEERFIELD PUBLISHING

1994

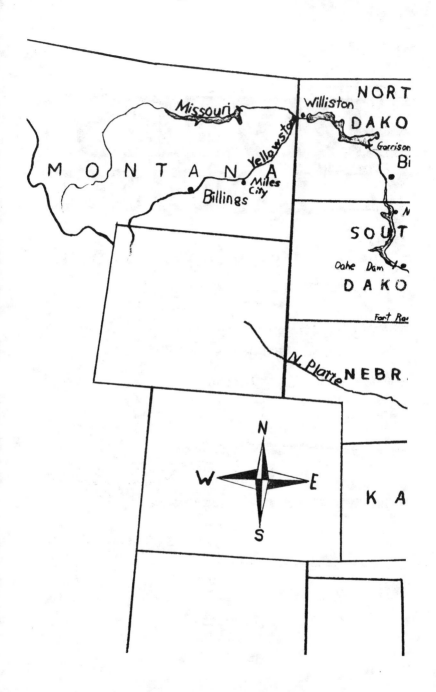

Also by Gordon Galloway

SCARS OF A SOLDIER
HILLBILLY POET
THE BULLDOG

Library of Congress Catalog Card Number: 98-93831
Copyright © 1998 by Gordon Galloway
All rights reserved
Printed in
The United States of America
Published by Deerfield Publishing Company
1613 130th Avenue
Morley, MI 49336
ISBN 0-9644077-3-6

Table of Contents

To honor a good friend, this book is dedicated to John Veneklasen. "And John, may there be lots of ducks in heaven," Scott.

Starting Point

I suppose that there is a certain time when most people sense the fleeting opportunity to lay down some milestones in their lives. To turn some dream into reality can be risky business, but in the long term, the thought of having the chance to do it, and then passing on the opportunity, is to me a very dismal thought. So, here I am in my mid-twenties, single but with a serious steady girl friend, money in the bank and a good job. All of this I'm exceedingly happy with. I look forward to getting married, raising kids, having a home and all the rest of the things people anticipate in life. It's just that before I do all that, I feel the need to break myself away from life's routine and pursue some dreams. Whether I am successful or not, I think my life will be more complete for having tried.

My first big adventure was to pedal my mountain bike from Grand Rapids, Michigan to New York to visit my sisters on Long Island, and then back to Michigan in time to be in a good friend's wedding, all in four weeks. This idea triggered some adverse opinions from about everyone. My mother thought the whole idea was unsafe as hell. If I wanted to do a long bike trip, it should be with a bunch of other bikers, not alone. Dad had no problem understanding why I wanted to do it alone; probably because he's a bit of a loner too, but he could foresee a host of problems that made such a trip questionable. At work they just made believe it wasn't going to happen until the time came to ask for the specific time off, which was during our busiest part of the year. The boss reluctantly agreed, with the hopes that I could trim my trip down some. When the foreman found out the boss OK'd my trip, he was so pissed he told me they'd probably eventually fire me. He then jumped in his truck and spun gravel as he left just to emphasize his anger with me.

My bike trip to New York and back went just fine, with lots of neat things happening to me. It's a trip I'd like to tell you about sometime but that's another story. What that trip really accomplished was to establish a certain credibility with everyone, that yes,

Scott can and will do what he sets out to do. So, in the fall of 1996 when I happened to mention to Dad that I was thinking about canoeing across Lake Michigan in 1997, he knew that I probably was serious about it. In no uncertain terms he tried to squelch that idea. He said that the lake was too damn cold, even in August. It could be extremely rough and dangerous with stormy weather, plus there was nothing to look at except water.

Eventually my thoughts for a Lake Michigan canoe crossing gave way to a river canoe trip, probably on the Mississippi. Dad didn't say anything more about the Lake Michigan thing. I imagine he thought if he brought it up and criticized the idea too much, I might do it just to prove I could. Parents sometimes perceive that type of attitude in their kids. Perhaps it's justified, too.

It was the second day of the 1996 deer hunting season. After being out in the cold all day hunting, we sat around the supper table visiting. I think everyone felt a little glow inside. Full stomachs, a couple deer hanging outside, a toasty warm kitchen and a sip or two of Yukon Jack to top things off. There used to be several of Dad's friends that came up from Detroit to hunt for a few days, but now it had dwindled down to Bob DeLanoy. Bob is a Northwest Airline Captain and has been coming up to hunt with us for as long as I can remember. He loves the outdoors as much as I do and I mentioned my thoughts of canoeing the Mississippi River the following summer. I could sense an internal sigh of relief from Dad. At least he perceived that I had abandoned that dumb idea of canoeing across Lake Michigan.

Bob listened with definite interest to my proposed trip. Then he said, "It sounds like a good trip, but did you ever consider taking on the Missouri? That's certainly an interesting river, especially with all the anniversary publicity commemorating Lewis and Clark's expedition." I went upstairs and brought down an atlas. We traced out the path of the Missouri and Bob pointed out different points of interest along the river. That night my next adventure was officially hatched, at least in my mind.

A Canoe

I knew that if I was going to tackle the Missouri River, I would need a really good craft to do it in. Most all of my previous experience to date was in the old fiberglass canoe Dad kept on the farm. Actually it belonged to Dad's brother, Uncle Garold. He had purchased it in the mid-fifties, but since Dad moved to the farm it had been stored there. Considering all this canoe had been through, and being over 40 years old, it was in very good condition. A few years ago I added some fiberglass to a weak area and painted it, so it looked even better now. The problem with this canoe was that it was too heavy for one man to carry any distance. I thought a kayak might be the best thing for my trip.

Late in the summer there was a big concentration of canoe and kayak dealers near a small pond by the Grand River in Grand Rapids. It was an opportunity for prospective buyers to try out and compare all the latest models available. After paddling several kayaks around the pond, it became apparent to me that a kayak was not going to be what I needed for this trip. It was much too confining, coupled with the fact that there just wasn't enough storage room. Camp gear and rations had to be stuffed down in some small cubbyholes. Also, it seemed that to keep the thing comfortably balanced, you needed to have a paddle in the water all the time. Kayaks are long, making them easy to move in a straight line, but more difficult to make quick turns with. I would concentrate my efforts on finding a worthwhile canoe instead.

From a canoe magazine dealership list, I sent away for as much information as I could get on canoes. Soon I had a pile of brochures to study what was available. The cheapest of the bunch was what I called the "Tupperware" variety. Made out of some kind of plastic, the shell was produced in large quantities, then shipped to the dealers who attached the seats and gunwale. They looked durable, and as I recall, were priced in the neighborhood of $600. The wood and canvas canoes really looked cool, but were expensive. They would probably be more vulnerable to damage from rock encounters on a river too. Repair might also be a problem. The best and lightest canoes were made out of a new material called Kevlar. It was supposed to be not only light, but strong and durable.

In the late fall I spent a lot of time at the library looking for books on canoeing. There was one on wintertime canoeing that caught my interest. That would certainly broaden my experience level, so I planned a couple of cold weather day trips to trace the origin of the river that crosses our farm, the Little Muskegon River.

The first trip went well. Dad dropped me off on the east branch of the Little Muskegon, north and west of Remus. On the second excursion he left me on the west branch in downtown Mecosta. The stream ran through a city picnic area and was very small but looked navigable. It was a pleasant day. The sun was out, but the temperature brisk, with snow on the ground. The pleasantness of the day soon left, for not far from the park I could see I was going to have problems. There just was too much brush along the way and the stream was too small. It was going to be slow and rough going. That was an understatement. It was terrible. There were trees down and my pace was that of a snail. It was getting late and I knew that I must make the little berg of Altona before dark. From there it would be easy going. I just didn't want to get caught in this brush at night. I had no provisions for an overnight stay either.

The stream widened some and I saw a tree down ahead. When I went around it I could immediately see there was another down in the opposite direction. I turned the canoe and lowered my head to shoot through the overhanging branches. In my haste I violated a golden rule and leaned into the current. The canoe immediately took on water, a lot of water. I was soaked to my thighs and wet above. The water wasn't as cold as I would have expected it to be. Perhaps it was because I had several layers of clothes on, including my long johns. My boots were also partially filled with water.

After I pulled the canoe up onshore, I took a good-sized limb and beat some small branches out of a dead pine tree. When I finished, I had a three-foot-high pile of brush. Fortunately, I always carry some matches with me in a zip-lock bag, so with some dry birch shavings for kindling, I soon had a roaring fire going.

I stripped down and put my clothes on the lower branches of the pine tree by the fire. In the meantime, I wrapped myself in a wool blanket which was dry. In an hour or so, my clothes were half dry. That had to be good enough; otherwise I wasn't going to get out of here before sunset. It was dark when I glided into Altona. I knew Dad would be worried, so I decided to end this trip. I walked to a house and called him. The man there volunteered to haul me home.

This, of course, was not an enjoyable trip, but in the end it gave me some confidence in my resolve to handle a bad situation. That resolve might be tested again next summer.

It was January before I got around to checking the phone directory yellow pages to see who the canoe dealers were in West Michigan. I called two and both had name brands available. One was in Holland, the other Muskegon. In the back of my mind I thought that December might be a slow month for these businesses; perhaps I could carve out a good deal with one of them.

The dealer in Holland had some really nice canoes, but was unenthusiastic about trying to sell me one. Maybe I didn't fit his image of a prospective buyer. I asked if I could try out a canoe. Yes, that was possible, but they would charge $20 to take it to the water for a demonstration. Of course the fee would be deducted from the overall cost if I bought one. These were expensive canoes. There didn't seem to be much available for under $1800 and the atmosphere wasn't right for any lower bargains to be negotiated. I got the impression they were used to dealing with a more elite class of customers. At heart I'm a miser, and I convinced myself I could do better.

Lumbertown was the dealer in Muskegon. This business was just a warehouse hidden in the industrial, low-rent section of Muskegon. I introduced myself to the owner, a fellow named Tom. I told him I needed a canoe for a long river trip in the summer, that I had the money to buy one and that his competition didn't seem interested in my business. Well, Lumbertown may not be impressive from the out-side, but the owner was interested in what I wanted and proceeded to spend an hour with me in his storage room, showing me the various types of canoes available and their advantages and disadvantages. Finally we narrowed the field down to four. Without blinking an eye, he called for a young helper to load up the canoes on their trailer. The employee took me to a long river channel that ends up in Lake Michigan. There, for an hour, I tried out each canoe.

There were lots of things to consider besides looks. Obviously, I needed something light that would have enough space for my gear, but each canoe handles differently in the water. If the bow or sides ride too high, the increased profile allows more exposure to the wind, which alters the paddler's intended course. Where one canoe could be easily pushed in a straight line through waves, it was more difficult to turn than a different make. Another canoe just seemed to be tippy. One of the canoes we brought along was the Bell Magic. In all respects, in my judgment, it was the most stable canoe. It was made of a Dupont-developed woven polymer called Kevlar. Not only was it light, with the canoe weighing around 40 pounds, it seemed strong and looked durable. You could hit an area with an object and it would absorb this energy through not just that spot, but a much larger area. It seemed that there wouldn't be as much chance of damage from an unexpected rock collision on the river. I found out later that I would need this durability.

When we arrived back at the business, I told Tom that I really liked the Bell Magic. He said the Bell was a good choice. It was a $1500 canoe, but he said I could have the demonstrator I had just used for $1350, plus a paddle. It seemed like a very good offer, however $1350 was still a lot of money. I wasn't mentally prepared to shell out over a thousand dollars for a canoe. I graciously thanked Tom for taking his time to show me the canoes. I just needed some time to consider the purchase. We parted with a handshake and he seemed as friendly when I left as when I had walked in his door earlier.

For the next month, I considered every option that would give me an acceptable canoe for less money. I bought a book on how to make your own Kevlar canoe, then called all around to find out where the materials were available. It ended up that the materials alone would amount to $500. That was a big investment, not including labor. I questioned whether or not I could make a canoe that would handle the way I wanted it to.

The most attractive canoe of course was the old canvas wood type. I considered buying an old one and fixing it up. There again, I wondered if such a craft could take the abuse it might receive in a fast river with rocks.

In mid-January, I called back over to Muskegon to see if the Bell Magic demonstrator was still there. The man that answered the phone said it was. I said, "I'm the guy that was over last month to try the Bell out. Tell the boss I have $1250 here in cash, that I will bring over in an hour if he'll sell it for that." "Just a minute," he replied. I could hear him relay my request to the owner who was away from the phone some distance. There were a few moments of silence, then a distant voice, "Tell him to come on over."

I made a trip to the bank and drove my '78 Dodge pickup over to Lumbertown where I counted out 12 hundred-dollar bills and a fifty. From there I drove back to Grand Rapids and the Grand River. I was intent on trying this baby out again, right away. There were large chunks of ice floating along. I asked myself if this was really smart. No life preserver was available, plus, there was a good possibility I could damage my new canoe on the ice chunks. My enthusiasm was dampened by good judgment. I took the canoe home and stored it in the garage. There were many other things that needed to be done in preparation for this trip. Plenty of time would be available later in the winter or spring to give the canoe a good workout.

Preparations

Because a good share of D.C. Byers' work is outside, there is a fair amount of time during the winter when I'm not working. This gave me a good opportunity to do some trip planning. I studied the path of the Missouri. At first, Great Falls, Montana, seemed like the logical place to start. I noticed there was a very large lake on the river, well over a hundred miles long behind Ft. Peck dam in northern Montana. There were several other big reservoirs on the Missouri too, starting in North Dakota, but perhaps I could at least avoid the Ft. Peck Lake if I instead started on the Yellowstone River in Billings, Montana. The Yellowstone becomes part of the Missouri just a few miles inside of North Dakota and it seemed like it might offer some nice scenery, a variation from what I could expect on the Missouri. There were no large dams to slow the current on the Yellowstone.

I had pretty well made up my mind to start the trip at Billings on the Yellowstone, but all these reservoirs on the Missouri worried me. There were three that looked to be 150 or more miles long each. I knew that the dams would slow the current in the reservoirs significantly, but how much? If there was no current, there would be a hell of a lot of paddling.

I tried my best to find some books or information on canoeing the Yellowstone and Missouri but could find nothing. The library folks showed me how to get on the internet through their computer. Still, I didn't have any luck learning about what to expect on these rivers.

The Lewis and Clark expedition books were gaining in popularity so I picked up one and started reading of their exploits. It was very interesting reading and I certainly admired their courage in tackling this river with its unexplored territories. As interesting as it was, that was a long time ago. The river had undergone a lot of changes. What I really wanted to read about was someone who had experienced canoeing on it recently.

There was one book that I located which did give me some needed insight into what it would be like to undertake such a trip. It wasn't about the Missouri; it was about one man's journey the length of the Mississippi. **MISSISSIPPI SOLO** was about this black man who, in the 80's, canoed from the Mississippi headwaters in Minnesota to its outlet in New Orleans. There was much to be learned from this man's experiences, a great deal from his mistakes.

Apparently Eddie Harris had an unexpected break from his job, and without much planning, he decided to tackle the Mississippi. He borrowed a canoe, packed his gear in plastic garbage bags, and in late October started his trip. From the problems this man had, I could start making a list of things I needed to avoid encountering similar unpleasant experiences on my trip.

One important item would be to come up with some kind of cover to keep rain and river water out of my canoe. There didn't appear to be any pre-made cover for this particular canoe, so I checked with several people who make boat covers. The least of the estimates for such a cover was around $500.

I got the name of a fellow in Minnesota who made good boat covers for a reasonable price. I called Cooks Custom Sewing and told the owner I had a Bell Magic canoe, could he make me a cover? He said that he hadn't made one for that particular brand, but with perimeter measurements he could make a stencil and do it, the cost $300. Mr. Cook said that there was a dealer in his area, but he couldn't guarantee when he would have the cover made. Six weeks later I received it in the mail. The snaps were included with the cover and those I had to install on the canoe myself. Sixty four holes I drilled in my new canoe. The cover fit perfectly. There was an opening right over my seat, with the capability to tighten the canvas around my waist. That $300 cover was one of the best investments I made.

To further protect my gear when it was unpacked from the canoe, I needed something better than plastic garbage bags. A lot of bags were available, all expensive. I ended up going to an Army surplus store for some inexpensive waterproof duffel bags.

My plan was to carry 10 days worth of provisions. In addition, I wanted to supplement my diet with some fresh meat. I needed an appropriate firearm to do a little hunting on the trip. I really didn't have anything particular in mind, just started looking around and asking people for advice.

John Veneklasen was a stroke victim whom my mother regularly cared for. He was a very successful Grand Rapids businessman and an avid duck hunter. In fact, John's stroke happened in a duck blind. He was crippled up, but his mind and speech were OK. Mom asked me to come over to his house one day and introduced us. Guess she figured I would be good therapy for him in his confined state, and perhaps his outdoor experience would benefit me.

From the very start of my trip planning, I involved John. In the later stages, I even brought all my equipment over for him to see. As much as I could, I wanted my adventure to be his adventure. Maybe it would bring a little brightness to the world of this dedicated outdoors man, whose life now revolved around a wheelchair and bed.

When I asked John what kind of gun he would suggest for my trip, he didn't have a specific recommendation, but did say a combination gun might be appropriate. I had no experience with over-under type guns, but there was a good-sized gun show in Grand Rapids, so I went to see what was available. I left with a combination barrel gun; a 22 rifle barrel on the top, and a 410 shotgun on the bottom, for $125.

This gun really turned out to be a poor investment. It was almost impossible to move the sliding firing pin from the shotgun position up to fire the 22. The trigger pull was extremely hard. On top of that, I found that 410 shells were very expensive, about $10 for 20. That was about double what 12 gauge shells sold for. When I fired it, I wasn't impressed with the 410 pellet pattern either. It sure didn't appear I would be bringing much game in with that gun. What I really wanted was to take this gun back to the dealer and get my money back. I remembered seeing a sign saying that all sales were final.

Even though I was convinced that this over-under would be mine forever, there soon was another gun show. With hopes of running into the guy that sold me this disappointment, I decided to take the gun to the show. About 30 seconds after I walked in with the gun on my shoulder, a man approached asking if I would like to sell it. I explained that I had purchased the gun a couple months back, and was here to return it if I could find the dealer.

After looking around some, I noticed a familiar lady sitting at a dealer's table. What luck. It was the wife of the guy that sold me the gun. At first she didn't recognize me.

"I bought this gun from your husband a couple of months ago. Maybe you remember; I'm the guy that needed a hunting gun for my canoe trip down the Missouri River next summer." That rang a bell; she did remember. Not too many minutes passed when her husband returned. I explained to him my dissatisfaction with the gun. His first response was to say that the gun was OK when he sold it to me. I was ready for that.

"This firing pin has been almost impossible to move to the 22 position from the day I took it home. Even a gunsmith told me he couldn't fix it. The trigger pulls too hard, and look at this; the front sight even easily falls off."

"Well, I'll take it home and fix it for you."

"No sir. I just want to return it and get my money back."

He obviously really didn't want to take the gun back. I don't think he wanted his reputation damaged either, so he gave me my money back.

The guy that first met me at the door came over, and seeing me without the gun, asked how I made out. I told him that I lucked out and got rid of it. Explaining the details of my planned trip, I said I was still in need of a gun. He said he collected over-unders and that he would help me look around the show for something. He also warned me that it's not unusual for dealers to bring junk to these shows, selling for top dollar with no return.

We scouted around to see what was available. There was a nice 22/12 gauge at one table. It just seemed like too much gun, too heavy for what I needed. Later I found a 22 magnum/20 gauge that looked just right. The dealer was asking $150. After leaving that dealer's space, my friend said, "Did you like that gun?"

"Yep," I replied. "A hundred fifty is a little much."

"You let me do the talking on this deal," he said.

I stood back as my friend returned to the dealer's table. He picked up the gun, closely examined it and said, "I really like this gun. It's a nice one. Would you take $120?"

"No, I need $150 for it."

"I'll give you $130, $150 is a little high."

"Well, I'll sell it to you for $140."

"How about splitting the difference, $135?"

"OK."

He called me back to the table.

"Give the man $135 and the gun is yours."

Fortunately I had an extra $15 in my billfold to go along with the $120 from the other rifle. What a deal. This was twice as good a gun as the other one. The magnum 22 had more punch as did the 20 gauge, plus the gun was small and light enough not to be a burden.

I thanked the man over and over for taking his time to help me. He wished me good luck, told me to have fun and be safe.

There were many people whose efforts were instrumental in the success of my trip. He was certainly high on that list.

The gun proved to be just what I needed. Twenty gauge shells were inexpensive to buy; on the other hand, the 22 magnum shells were as expensive as the 410 shells. That I could put up with, as the gun worked perfectly.

This trip would undoubtedly take at least a couple of months to complete. That would be a considerable amount of paddling. How much I enjoyed the journey would probably, to a large extent, depend on how comfortable I was, so a good seat was a must. There were several kinds of seats on the market. What I ended up with was the Crazy Creek canoe chair. It would snap upright or recline way back on my gear. I can't say enough good things about how well it worked.

Everything was slowly coming together.

III

Details

It is very easy for me to temporarily avoid those situations that may cause me difficulty. I believe it's called procrastination. Remembering the reluctance of my employer to give me time off last year, and the anger of my foreman when they gave it to me, I did not look forward to putting forth the request again. When Dad asked if I had made a move yet, invariably the time of potential confrontation would be slid back another month.

As soon as the water was clear of ice, I had the Bell Magic out for a spin. It performed very well. My only reservation was with the paddle that came with the deal. With a single paddle, there is much more effort expended in switching sides to keep the ship going straight. Also everytime the paddle crosses the center, water drips off. My investment in this trip was increasing rapidly, but everything thus far seemed necessary. For $117 I bought a new double bladed paddle. It seemed expensive, however it would prove to be my very best investment. Not only did it end up saving me energy from not having to continually switch sides, it improved my overall speed and ability to handle tricky situations faster.

Transportation from Michigan to Billings, Montana with my canoe and gear was a problem that needed to be solved. Dad had vacation in October, so he would pick me up in St. Louis, Missouri, where I would end my trip. He also said that if there was no other means available he would also make sure that I got to Billings. It was really asking a lot to have him do both.

My girl friend, Renae, came to the rescue. She said that she would be happy to drop me off in Billings. Afterwards, she would continue on out to Oregon and visit a cousin. Renae would graduate from Grand Valley State University in the spring and she figured it would be a nice trip to celebrate her graduation.

A friend at work introduced Renae to me a few years ago and it seemed to be working into a good match. Whenever we both could get days off together, and the weather was good, I would take her up to the farm for some canoeing, hunting or just hiking back by the river.

If a person moves slowly and quietly in the woods there is a lot to see and pleasures to experience. The sounds of the various birds, the movements of animals, just being part of nature's undisturbed peace can be a real inspiration. Renae seemed to enjoy all of this just as much as I did.

On our trips together down the Little Muskegon I tried to introduce Renae to all the things that had given me so much enjoyment in the past. She was attentive to everything. She easily picked up the skills needed to maneuver the canoe and had an uncanny ability with firearms. From the 22 rifle to the deer rifle, shotgun, 22 pistol and even Dad's 38 revolver, she handled all of them confidently. I even checked her out on the chain saw, cutting up some firewood for Dad. She had lots of sore muscles the next day, but there was little complaining.

At first we made plans to have another couple go with us out west. Renae has a small car so it looked like, with all of my gear, we would really be crowded. The other couple eventually backed out anyway. I really didn't want Renae driving by herself after dropping me off, so we needed to find at least one other person to go. It wasn't long before we had a very willing volunteer, Aunt Shelby. Aunt Shelby was in her late 50's. She recently retired from Chrysler in Cleveland and moved up to live with her brother in Ionia. In her younger years, she was an active outdoors person who enjoyed camping and participated in everything from white water rafting to mountain horseback riding. She had toured all around the United States.

Shelby was very enthusiastic about the trip. She immediately immersed herself into all the planning, and even mapped out a trip for her and Renae to the western states after dropping me off. She was also insistent that we use her car, which was new, roomier and would be air-conditioned. The transportation problem was solved.

From what I could figure, it would probably take around two months to complete my journey. That was based on an average of about 40 miles a day. I was confident that on some parts of the river the current alone should take me that fast. And with some paddling I could increase that by 50%. Maybe I could even double the mileage. What I didn't know was what speed I would be capable of on the many miles of reservoirs.

Dad's vacation would be over the last week in October, so for me to arrive in St. Louis by then, I would have to leave Billings, Montana the last part of August. At least that would allow me most of the summer to work for the company.

I cautiously approached one of the supervisors and explained in detail about my proposed trip. What I was after was his opinion on how much hassle I was going to create, and the best way to approach the boss. There was also the hope that he might leak my plans to the boss, so I wouldn't catch him completely by surprise.

It was in late July when I finally gathered my courage to officially ask for the time off from work. The boss quietly listened as I spilled forth with the pertinent details of the trip. The bottom line was that I felt compelled to do some things in my life while I was single and young enough to really enjoy them. That was my selling point. Even if he didn't want me to take time off during our busy season, I thought he would appreciate what I wanted to accomplish.

I think the other supervisor must have laid the groundwork for my visit, because the boss didn't seem real surprised. There wasn't any detectable anger in his manner either, only a slight bit of impatience when he said, "Well, Scott, how long will it take you to paddle your ass back to Michigan?"

During the summer months I regularly had my canoe on the Grand River trying to build up my body for the big trip. There was also plenty of effort expended trying to learn details of what I would encounter along my route.

From internet photos, I could see what the country around the start of the Yellowstone looked like. It was quite scenic. I called out to some campgrounds on the Yellowstone and Missouri Rivers and yes, people did canoe out there, but it didn't seem like it was a regular occurrence. My gut feeling was that I really didn't know much about these rivers, or what I was getting into.

In late June, Renae had some research to do at the Michigan State Library. I drove her there, and while she worked on her project, I looked for new information on my trip. Finally I hit pay dirt.

There was an expedition planning guide that mentioned the two rivers. It was a technical manual, but it did give flow rates, weather patterns, obstacles and difficulties of certain areas. I welcomed any tidbit of background information that would make me feel more confident in what I was doing. I made photocopies of much of the information so that I could study it at home.

One thing the expedition planner recommended was that, for 200 miles south of Bismarck, the route was fit for expert canoers only. Specifically it said, 'dangerous, poor canoeing, big water.' That sure didn't build any confidence in me. I certainly wasn't any kind of an expert with a canoe. Plus, I just couldn't pick up my canoe and walk around 200 miles of rough water. I had no intention of calling off this trip for any reason, but I can assure you, there was lots of uneasiness buried in my subconscious core.

Heading West

We all met at the farm on Friday, mid-morning. Renae and I drove up from Grand Rapids with my canoe and gear in the back of the pickup. Shelby arrived with a car storage carrier on top of her Chrysler and her trunk quite full. Notorious for her fine baked goods, Shelby had lots of cookies, muffins and other goodies packed for the trip.

The farm was a little out of the way to start our journey, but I wanted to leave the truck there, plus it just seemed like a fitting place to begin the trip. My stepmother, Mary Ann, and sister Staci put together a great breakfast while we got everything packed away in Shelby's car. Boy, were we loaded, trunk, car carrier, and back seat on one side. With several bungee cords, I secured the canoe onto the car carrier.

We had said good-bye to mother Gwynn in Grand Rapids. She had made her contribution to things she thought I needed on the trip. Dad was out of state with the airlines, but he called after breakfast to wish me luck.

Everything was finally stowed away and it was time to say good-bye. After some pictures and hugs, we were on our way, me driving.

Our farm is on the corner of 130th Ave. and Jefferson Road. Turning west on Jefferson, I took one more nostalgic look out the right window at our house and farm buildings. With an aggressive push to the gas pedal, Shelby's new Chrysler quickly accelerated. We were on our way. Less than a quarter of a mile from the corner, I was nearing 45 mph and the canoe was starting to fly off the car.

There was no question in my mind what had happened. The canoe was light and as the car picked up speed, wind gathered under the canoe, creating some strong lift. The bungee cords, which were not strong enough to hold the canoe down, began to stretch, allowing it to be lifted. I was immediately on the brakes to stop this action, but it was too late. The canoe came down on my side hitting the pavement hard. It dragged along until I had the car stopped.

My brand new canoe now had numerous scratches on it. Part of the gunwale was broken off. I surveyed the damage, concluding that it was, for the most part, cosmetic. Fortunately, there were no cars coming in the opposite direction to run into it either. I was lucky. Had I been going faster and not noticed it coming off, there might have been some real serious damage.

Shelby went back to the house to find something to secure the canoe. When she couldn't find what I wanted, I left the girls with the canoe and returned for some good tie-down rope. When I came back, I could see Steve Stilson's red truck parked alongside the road. Many years ago Steve had gone with us on our first overnight trip down the Little Muskegon River.

I started to slowly pull up parallel to the canoe. Renae stepped out of the way. Aunt Shelby tried to step backward, forgetting the canoe was right behind her. She lost her balance, went backward into the canoe, then she and the canoe ended up rolling over into the ditch. I thought she might be hurt, but she got up laughing, dusting herself off. Steve Stilson was taking in the whole scene and enjoying it immensely. Of course, he had lots of questions as to where this operation was headed.

What had originally seemed like the ideal grand departure for my adventure was more like a scene from one of Chevy Chase's vacation movies.

I guess I had already mentally prepared myself for mishaps on this trip, for I wasn't upset and could see the humor in the whole thing. If this was the worst thing that would happen, I was sure everything would work out OK.

This time I tied the canoe down to the front and rear of the car; so tight that when I eventually was ready to take it off in Billings, it took 20 minutes to untie.

My intention was to get to Billings, Montana as quickly as possible. Renae and I took turns doing most of the driving. Of course there were several meal and stretch stops, but we kept up a good clip across the states on I-90. We drove all through Friday evening and early Saturday morning. Sometime after midnight, we entered Mitchell, South Dakota, home of the Corn Palace. That and Mt. Rushmore were two attractions which were mandatory stops on the way out. Well the Corn Palace was nice; lots of mosaics made out of colorful Indian corn. But, at this time, 3 a.m. in the morning, my enthusiasm for being a tourist was zilch. We pressed on and finally at 5 a.m. pulled into a rest stop in Chamberlain, S.D.

We slept in the car for 2 hours or so. Shortly after daybreak, I woke the girls up. They went into the restrooms to freshen up a bit. It seemed like they were taking a long time in there so I took a little walk around the area. There was a unique Tepee monument erected on a high point nearby. I walked to the top of a hill to get a good look at the surrounding scenery. At the crest of the hill I gazed over to the west and there, with mist rising above it, was the Missouri River. I hadn't checked the map and didn't realize we were even close yet. This was a beautiful river. It looked better than I had pictured it would be in my mind. I was transfixed. The river flow was so smooth, the countryside so gorgeous. I was exhilarated. This would be the ultimate trip. I took a deep breath of the fresh morning air and was instantly refreshed from the long hours of driving.

Renae and Shelby were waiting by the car wondering what happened to me. I called them over to see the river. They were equally impressed. All of a sudden everything about this trip was taking on a new reality. I couldn't wait to get started, but first there was Mt. Rushmore.

From the start of the trip Shelby had been telling us about how impressive Mt. Rushmore was. Unfortunately the Mt. Rushmore Shelby remembered was the park 15 or 20 years ago. Things had changed. Apparently, there used to be more trees, rustic footpaths and less tourists. Now much of the land had been cleared. There was a four-lane road leading to the attraction; a three-story parking ramp, a huge gift shop where everything was stamped with the Rushmore logo and asphalt trails.

Shelby was totally disgusted. She was ready to leave immediately. Her beautiful memories of this place had been destroyed by the modernization put in place to accommodate the increasing number of tourists.

We were studying the presidents' faces with a pair of binoculars. When they were offered to Shelby she refused them. "I've seen this place and I'm not impressed. Are you guys ready to go?" After a couple of pictures we left.

On Saturday night we got a motel room. After driving so long, we needed a chance to get a good night's sleep. We were about a three-hour drive from Billings and I wanted to be fresh to start my trip.

The first thing I wanted to do here in Billings was finish filling my supply list. There were things I could get here that weren't worth hauling all the way from Michigan; gas for my cookstove, more food and shotgun shells. After shopping, we spent almost a half-hour driving around looking for a public ramp area to put the canoe in.

For some reason I was getting nervous. I never thought I'd be worried about doing something I really wanted to do, but my stomach was beginning to tighten up. Even though I hang off tall buildings at work, guess I wasn't the tough guy I thought I was.

We finally found the small boat ramp and I got my first look at the Yellowstone. I was terrified.

The Yellowstone

August 24th to August 27th

The Yellowstone was about the same width as the Grand River going through Grand Rapids. The similarity ended there. Boy, was this river cranking. It reminded me of the treacherous wild jungle rivers I had seen in movies.

I was really nervous. There were two lively conversations going on in my head. One voice was saying, "Man, let's get the hell out of here, you can't do this!" The other voice was trying to calm me down.

"Don't worry. You'll learn how to handle this current. We drove all the way out here; there's no turning back now."

There was an uncomfortable silence as I stood there with the two girls watching this raging river. A lone kayaker went whizzing by and was out of sight in a few seconds. You could actually see the change in elevation as the river dropped 8 to 10 feet within a half-mile. There were also logs and limbs going by. All of us knew that old Scott would have his hands full out there. I didn't want to act panicky, and they didn't want to make me nervous, so other than a few oohs and ahs, we just started making ourselves busy unpacking my stuff from the car. Once we had everything laid out on the ground I started organizing it so that the things I would need quickly would be available. Less essential items would be more towards the bottom of the canoe, like the sail kit I had. On this river the sail was the absolute last thing I needed.

Trying to act confident, I buried myself into the business of packing the canoe. There was no ignoring this river, though. The knot in my stomach kept growing. It had grown from baseball to softball size and with each fleeting glance at this monster it was getting bigger.

The girls had really planned a nice picnic lunch for my departure; shrimp, homemade banana bread and cookies, a great spread. What a nice way to celebrate the start of my trip. Or, the more I thought about it, maybe more like a last supper.

While the girls cleaned up after our lunch, I put the last odds and ends in the canoe and started to snap my canvas cover on. Meanwhile a Montana conservation officer drove up. He walked over to where I was working by the canoe.

"Gonna do a little canoeing?"

"Yep."

"Where ya headed, down to Custer?" Custer was the first town of any size about 40 miles down the river.

"Nope, I'm going all the way to St. Louis."

"Well the river is a little higher than normal but you look like an experienced canoer. I'm sure you'll have a lot of fun."

Looks are really deceiving I guess, or else he was just trying to reassure me. As far as the river being a little high, I found out later that due to the heavy snow runoff, it was three feet higher than flood stage. He didn't mention that. He did tell me that there were a lot of fish in the river and I should trail a line behind the canoe to get some fresh fish for meals.

I tried to find out as many details about the river as I could from this guy. He told me about the Huntley Diversion Dam, which was 20 or so miles down the river. I would have to portage around that.

Before the officer left, he asked me a favor.

"We had a teenager that fell in the other night and drowned, but haven't found the body yet. Would you please keep an eye out for it? Could have washed up onshore someplace down river."

Finding a body didn't bother me, but knowing the river had the capability to kill a teenager didn't exactly add to my confidence. I told him I would do my best to watch for the body and thanked him for the good information. He walked back to his car and drove away.

It was time to start. Everything was ready and the canoe was perched on the water's edge waiting for me to climb in and take control. Now there was no thought of turning around in my mind, but lots of apprehension.

I gave Shelby a good-bye hug and thanked her for the ride out. Renae was teary eyed. I held her tightly in my arms and told her I'd see her in a couple of months. I said that she and Shelby would have a great vacation, that I loved her and would miss her. Renae gave me a half smile and a passionate kiss and we parted. As she said good-bye I could hear trembling in her voice.

The girls wanted to get some pictures as I started down the river. There was a dirt road that followed the river for a ways, so they headed for the car as I pushed out into the fast current.

They drove down a half-mile or so and barely got into position for a couple pictures as I went by. I tried to back paddle to slow my drift, but finally blew Renae a kiss, waved a few times and they were out of sight. I was alone and frightened, but also excited about being on my way. My heart was pounding in my chest and adrenalin was flowing like the river.

As the river left Billings there were a few houses in sight, then civilization quickly disappeared.

The riverbanks were covered with cottonwoods on both sides. Occasionally there was a clearing where a cow pasture bordered the river. It was very green and pretty, however the speed of the river left little time for leisure sightseeing. Safety was paramount in my mind. I wanted to keep my canoe and my body intact until the arch at St. Louis was in sight. As I hit the first logjam, the current was doing some crazy things. I just told myself to continue paddling and keep one paddle in the water.

The Bell Magic handled perfectly in the fast water. It seemed like the craft felt right at home on this river. She was responsive and waiting for me to guide her on this journey.

In about a mile or so there was a place out of the main current where I could pull up onshore. There was something else that I needed to do at the beginning of this trip. I was alone, but I didn't want to be alone. I knelt down onshore and asked the Lord to watch over me, keep me safe.

As I gazed out on this swift river, I thought about the hundreds, maybe thousands, of people that had been down the river before me.

This was Lewis and Clark's return route. Before them only the Indians and after them more explorers, trappers and finally the pioneers. In a small way I was part of this river's history too. Although it was a dangerous river, I didn't want to look at it as an adversary or an obstacle. The Indians consider different parts of their environment as family. The river was a brother and that's how I wanted to perceive it.

In a small circle of rocks I sprinkled down a pile of pipe tobacco. A light wispy smoke curled up from the burning tobacco and its odor filled the fresh river air. Maybe the spirits of the river would take notice and bless my journey as I had asked my God to do. I was certain that there were forces out there affecting my life each day. It was not all chance. The knot in my stomach was gone. There was a calm within me. I was ready to do this and I knew it was right.

On the way once more, I thought how I'd handle things if the drowned teenager's body appeared. If it wasn't onshore I'd have to get a rope attached to it and somehow get it to shore, then find a phone and call someone.

Not far from Billings I discovered a whole bunch of bodies: auto bodies. There was a long string of 50's and 60's hulks with a cable running through them, all embedded in the riverbank. The cable was attached to a cement pylon at each end. The purpose of this lineup was obviously aimed at keeping the river from stealing any more of that person's property and the junk cars were doing a good job of holding the soil in place. In other unprotected areas it wasn't unusual to see a building ready to fall into the river. At one point, a red barn was collapsing into the river and the house wasn't far behind. The river was a notorious thief of property, carving away the banks as it determined its own route.

With all the environmental rules and regulations in place, that form of erosion control was probably short-lived. I wondered if the crankcases had been drained of oil or the batteries removed. They sure didn't spare the chrome in those days. I could imagine that antique car collectors would like to get their hands on them for spare parts. Some were in pretty good shape.

It seems that a river reflects and amplifies sounds. I would always tell everyone I canoed with that their voices would carry down the river, alarming the wildlife. If they were quiet there was a lot of animals and birds to be seen. On this river there was another sound that brought back that sinking feeling in my guts. The sound of rushing water. This high fast current had picked up a lot of debris, forming numerous logjams on the outside of bends. The water would boil underneath the piles of logs and limbs causing a sucking sound. I had no intention of being nailed against or drawn underneath, so when one came into view I would paddle like mad to keep a safe distance. I was very cautious and would routinely get out and check if I heard disturbing river noise ahead.

I knew from my map that the Huntley Diversion Dam would be coming up soon. The officer said I'd have to portage around it, but otherwise I didn't know what to expect. Soon I began to hear the distant roar of water. Not the same as that sound created by a logjam.

The current seemed to be slowing down now. Signs appeared on each side of the river telling boaters to turn around or go ashore. The signs didn't say which side to get out on. I remember someone saying to the right is usually the right choice. I stayed on the right side straining to see the dam down river, but could see nothing. I was looking for a boat ramp. There was a concrete wall on this side and no place to get out. The river noise was getting louder and louder.

I was getting antsy. Finally I stood up in the canoe to see ahead. There, less than 600 feet away, was the drop-off. I sat back down and paddled for all I was worth toward the other side. The noise was increasing. There was mist created by the water falling below the dam. I was making good speed but losing ground. It looked like the current would take me over before I reached the other side. I had to paddle harder! Aiming the canoe slightly upstream, I summoned up a quantity of adrenalin from someplace for an additional last minute desperate effort to avoid the drop. It seemed like I could hear the canoe paddles cracking from the force of my pull. Seconds before going over I made the other shore, grabbed a drift log, got one foot out and pulled the canoe onshore away from the river's sucking sound. My one leg was shaking so badly I could hardly control it.

I walked to the tip of the embankment and looked down. It was at least a 9 to 10 foot drop-off. The water was boiling below. On the opposite shore downstream there were three fishermen who had been watching my efforts. They all had their fishing poles tucked under their arms and were giving me a round of applause. Talking to them afterwards, they said they were sure I was going over. My heart was still pounding hard for 5 to 10 minutes after I reached shore.

It took me eights trips on 100 yards of jagged rocks to get my stuff around the dam. I considered pushing off again, but decided against it. With a few hours of daylight left, I found a nice sand bar to set up my tent on. The conservation officer had advised me to pull out early when I found a good campsite. That was good advice for I had a full day and was pretty tired. Since I hadn't taken a shower in 48 hours, I walked to the canal part of the diversion dam, stripped and bathed in the ice-cold water from the mountain snow melt.

The next morning I was up early, cooked a hearty breakfast, broke camp and was on my way. It was a glorious morning with the coolness of the river bathed in sunshine.

There were lots of fishermen on the Yellowstone. All would wave when they saw me. Sometimes I would pull out and visit for awhile. Each time I tried to find out as much as I could about any obstacles ahead.

There was a place on my map called POMPEYS PILLAR. That shouldn't be too far away. A one lane bridge was visible ahead with a fisherman underneath. I asked him if he knew where Pompeys Pillar was.

"Yep, it's 100 yards right over that hill. You could almost see it from here if it weren't for the trees." I pulled the canoe up onshore and headed for the hill.

Pompeys Pillar is a 100' rock column in a farmer's field. I could easily see it as I came over the hill. It's the only place where they can definitely fix a Lewis and Clark stop. Lewis carved his name there and the year, 1804. The carving is protected by bulletproof glass now, plus a motion sensor that sets off an alarm if anyone messes with it. Before the man-made protection was installed, an overhead outcropping of rock protected it from weather. There was a gift shop there and an attendant.

As I walked back to the canoe I felt a little more a part of history. I was actually on the Lewis and Clark route. In my spare time I began reading more about their expedition. I wished I had read the whole story before I left home.

I felt more comfortable on the river now, however because of the fast current and logjams, there was no point that I could kick back and really relax.

The next town was 30 miles away, so until then I would be away from civilization. In some ways, this made me feel rather vulnerable. Who knows what could happen out here and how would anyone find out other than discovering part of my stuff or my body floating down river. This was not a real worry, but those thoughts did linger in the back of my mind. When there was a scary moment they would make a haunting return.

The less I saw of other human beings and the civilized world, the more I felt a part of my natural surroundings. There were lots of water birds to observe. Eagles were a common sight. Although I didn't see them often, I knew the beaver were busy all along the river. They weren't the least bit hesitant to take on the large cottonwoods for their dam construction, either. Many of those trees had been heavily girdled by the beaver and would eventually come down. I was amazed at their patience and persistence in achieving the goals that had been firmly established in their thought process. They certainly couldn't be considered dumb little creatures.

The town of Custer seemed right near the river on the map, so I decided to camp there and walk into town to call home. After a couple miles of walking, I still hadn't reached town. There was a small farmhouse, so I stopped there and rapped on the door. An old lady that looked to be about 75 years old opened the door. Her smile told me she welcomed company and was not threatened by my presence. I introduced myself as I would do a hundred times over on this trip.

"Hi. I'm Scott Galloway and I'm canoeing the Yellowstone and Missouri Rivers from Billings to St. Louis. I was looking for a place to call home."

Well, without hesitation, that kind old lady invited me right in. She pointed to the phone and headed for the kitchen to get a cold drink for me.

I was really looking forward to hearing a familiar voice from home and I did, but it was the voices on two answering machines.

I knew that everyone would be anxious to hear from me, but I couldn't expect them to hang around the phone 24 hours a day waiting for me to call. It was a disappointment though. I left a brief message so at least they would know I was safe and having a good time.

The old lady brought out a tall glass of grape juice and sat down to visit. I started the conversation by asking questions about her. She said that her husband had died several years ago and this was the place that they had farmed together for many years. I can't remember what she said they used to grow, the crop wasn't familiar to me. Even though she was alone, she intended to continue living here where the good memories were, at least as long as her health held up. She didn't say whether or not they had children.

I'm sure she would have liked to talk longer, but I wanted to get my camp set up before dark. I thanked her for her kindness and left. The old lady probably didn't have many people to visit with. Because of that thought I felt guilty. Our generation just doesn't take enough time to visit with or appreciate old folks. I can easily see this failing in other young people and now I can see it in myself as well.

I had used my river sandals for the walk to the farmhouse. They had rubbed against my toes and the tops of my toes were raw. It would take two weeks for them to heal. From then on I used hiking boots and left the sandals under the seat.

Just before light the next morning, I slid the canoe into the water. It seemed like a reasonably safe stretch of river and I wanted to be in the water when the sun came up.

It was a little misty as light came to the river. For awhile the terrain delayed a direct view of the sun's splendor, but a vast array of yellow and gold soon made its way through the cottonwoods. The birds seemed to respond with their happy sounding chirps and screams. The animals were already there too, ready to end a busy night or start a new day depending on their habits. A mule deer was at the shore for a drink, a red fox was sniffing around onshore. The fox noticed me, but I was still. At that distance I probably looked like another tree floating along. The canoe was gliding right towards him. He put his head back down and continued investigating with his nose. When I was less than 100 feet away, he quickly looked up again, determined I was more than a log, then left the area.

It was somewhere around Hysham where I met the two Indian boys. There was a small rapids there with an irrigation canal. Coming up the river I hadn't noticed the car, so apparently they just arrived. I waved and pulled up onshore to introduce myself.

In the course of our conversation, they said that they wished they had remembered to bring along a lantern to fish for catfish. I said that I had one they could use, as I was planning to set up camp here for the night. In fact, if they would run me into town for some supplies I might procure some beer and go fishing with them. They needed no convincing.

The evening turned out great. We ate beef jerky, drank beer, visited and caught catfish until 2 a.m. The catfish were big enough to snap the lines half of the time, but we did land several 3 to 4 pounders which were probably 20 inches or so long.

The boys had graduated from high school, but they didn't have jobs yet. One had inherited $20,000 from his grandfather when he turned 18 years old. He had been busy spending it for the last couple of years. Eight thousand dollars went for a hot rod that now had a blown engine. I'm not sure where the rest went, but he only had $2,000 left. It didn't seem like these young men had any plan in life. They were just living in a tent, riding around different places fishing. If he would have left that twenty thousand or at least part of it in the bank, he would have a nice investment building interest for the future. I felt like delivering a lecture, but I thought otherwise. I'm the guy that risked his job to take two months off to canoe a river. Probably criticism could easily be leveled at me. Short-lived as it might be, maybe their lifestyle was OK too.

Fishing is not one of my big pleasures in life, but I did have fun that night. I hadn't cleaned catfish before so they gave me a quick lesson. I'd always thought catfish had barbs or stingers in their whiskers. Instead I found out that at the tip of the body fins a small sharp bone sticks out. If they flip around and catch you with it, the venom secreted through it will cause swelling. The safest place is to hold them by the belly, leave the skin on and just fillet them. In a matter of a few minutes the fish were done. It was obvious they had cleaned fish a few hundred times before.

We sat around the fire talking for several hours. That's when they told me about all the legends of that area. The boys said good-bye and left about 3 a.m. I crawled into my sleeping bag and things seemed to be spinning a bit. It had been a long day, with a few too many beers at the end of it.

For breakfast the next morning I rolled the four catfish in flour, seasoned and fried them in my skillet with oil. Along with scrambled eggs they were absolutely delicious. So good in fact, that I ate all of them. My stomach was uncomfortable for quite awhile that morning.

There was no shortage of ducks along the river. I decided it was time for the great white hunter to put some fresh meat on the table. I had the gun handy with two 20 gauge and two 22 magnum shells. The rest of the ammunition was packed away.

The duck was onshore maybe a couple hundred feet away. My first shot was a mere dusting. Just enough to keep him from getting airborne. I felt bad. I don't like to just wound game. The current was taking me downstream. I had to reload another 20 gauge shell and then paddle back upstream for another shot. The duck would dive underwater for 30 seconds, then back up. I got off another shot which hit, but still didn't kill him. A 22 shell caught one wing and he couldn't dive anymore. Reload, paddle – still I couldn't get closer than 30 feet from him. With a hit in the other wing, he was still scrambling in the water and I was out of ammunition.

Finally the stream carried the duck close enough that I could grab him and put him out of his misery. The whole thing was downright disgusting. The shot in the 20 gauge shells was too small to be very effective at long range. I vowed that from that time on I would only take close sure shots, and have extra ammunition available. I didn't want a replay of that incident.

That night I boiled the duck for an hour with spices, then fixed some noodles for duck spaghetti. It wasn't great, but certainly edible. I did have to be careful chewing as there was plenty of lead in this bird.

From that camp outside of Forsyth, I again called home to talk to the answering machines. Told them I was having the time of my life. Only a sore back, shoulders and butt detracted from my happiness. The weather was beautiful, the scenery great, the people were friendly and the river was allowing me to pass. That message should give the home folks some peace of mind. And it was all true. The trip was going just fine, except I thought that with the fast current I should be making more than my usual 40 to 50 miles per day.

Miles City was the first large city right on the river. I pulled up to a boat ramp area that said NO CAMPING and set up my tent anyway. I was out of clean clothes. I did my best to wash in the river and hang the clothes out to dry. Several people stopped to visit and hear about my trip. It seemed like I was saying the same thing, answering the same questions over and over. But everyone along this river appeared to have a genuine interest in me and what I was doing. Sometimes life is so busy that the dreams of adventure become fulfilled through someone else rather than a person being able to do it oneself. Maybe in some way my trip was just a little bit their trip.

Usually people had some story about their life they wanted to share with me. First they'd ask about me, then lead the conversation into what they really wanted to talk about. It happened so many times it became typical.

A guy in an old Ford pickup came around. I told him I needed to walk for supplies and could use some directions. He offered me a ride to the store and I accepted. He was even kind enough to wait outside and furnish my ride back.

That night I hung my flashlight in the top of the tent and tried to write some letters. A strong breeze eventually turned into an all-night rain, but I was now cozy in my sleeping bag.

With a good night's rest, clean clothes and french toast for breakfast, I would be ready to start the last half of my Yellowstone journey. I felt mentally prepared. Soon I fell into a sound sleep.

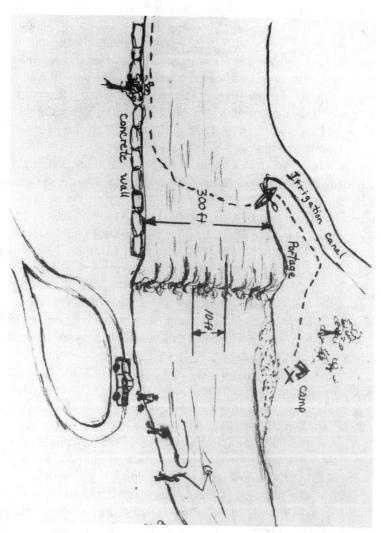

Huntley Diversion Dam

concrete wall

300 ft

10 ft

Irrigation Canal

Portage

Camp

The Yellowstone – Part II

August 28th to September 2nd

Eastern Montana has a dryer climate and away from the river the hills were rocky and the ground covered with sagebrush. Near the river everything was usually green. Sometimes that would change. One side of the river shoreline would be dry looking like the countryside and the other lush green. Where it was green there were mosquitoes, and they could be real bothersome at night.

From what I could tell the speed of the river was not changing. My map depicted the elevation changes at cities and points along the way. It was obvious the river was on its way downhill. Yes, I was learning to handle it, but I could not relax my awareness of its danger. There was no doubt in my mind that, if for one minute I wasn't very careful in maneuvering the canoe, the river would quite willingly gobble me up.

After Miles City I saw no human beings for almost 40 miles. Prior to this, there were long stretches where I didn't see any fishermen or campers, but I would see trains because the tracks weren't far from the river.

The trains were very long and most of them were hauling coal. One of the fishermen I talked with was a retired train engineer. He said that there were big deposits of coal out here, but it was of a very poor grade. The trains carry this coal to plants where the impurities are burned out, then it goes to the electrical power plants for fuel.

Like everyone else the train engineers would wave to me. There were no other canoes or boats on the river so this lone canoeist was something unusual. Perhaps I represented a spirit of freedom and adventure that for a few moments gave some brightness to their daily routine. At least I hoped that was the case. I did feel that I was doing something special.

Being our national symbol, I should have been in awe of all the eagles around. I wasn't that impressed. The pelicans were the birds that fascinated me the most. On some of the river islands there might be up to a hundred congregated. They always started their flight from the water.

The pelicans are heavy birds with wing spans that look to be five to eight feet. To get airborne, they start flapping those big wings and then, as they start to come up, it looks like they are actually walking on water. When their feet are off the water, they tuck them behind, but rarely would these big birds get more than a few inches above the water. They'd flap those big wings and then glide, flap them some more and glide on.

Sometimes when they saw me, there would be some brave pelicans resting on a log that were reluctant to hit the water and fly. Probably they'd just had a good meal and didn't want to be disturbed. Routinely I would head the canoe right towards them so eventually they'd be alarmed enough to head to the water for flight. It was pure entertainment watching them get airborne.

There was another really neat bird, but it was very small, like a sparrow. I believe it is called a crey. It could float on the water just like a duck and would hunt in a group of 10 or more about 30 feet above the water. When it spotted a minnow, that bird would go straight up then right back down in a steep dive with its wings tucked behind it. At the surface of the water there was no hesitation. I watched them repeatedly go headfirst into the water from a dive, at least once every three or four minutes. When they did get a fish, it was up to a tree limb for the meal. It sure seemed to me that after a day of that kind of fishing they would have a severe headache.

The beaver had been working all along the river, but as they are nocturnal, rarely did I see one. If I paddled after sunset or before sunrise, I would hear them hit the water and know that they were there.

At lunch one day I could smell something dead nearby. Upon investigation I found an otter's decaying body, so I knew that otters lived out here too. What I expected to see was lots of range cattle and some horses, but they just weren't near the river.

On a regular basis I had been knocking down some ducks to supplement my diet. The day before I had made some duck soup, which was very good. I tried as many ways as I could think of to prepare them to keep some variety in my meals.

As I said before, after Miles City I went the whole day without seeing a soul. Finally out in the middle of a desolated area where the Powder River joins the Yellowstone, there was a lone fisherman. He had several lines in the water with a four-wheel-drive vehicle parked close by. Probably I was disrupting this man's solitude, but I looked forward to some human interaction.

The guy was a college professor and looked a little geeky, but was pleasant. He told me that there were a lot of fossils in the rocks around there, so after a short visit I meandered around looking for some. When I picked up one loose layer of clay, what I found instead of a fossil was a big old yellow scorpion.

The scorpion measured about four inches across. With a little stick I poked him a bit to see how he used his stinger and claws. With a claw he grabbed the stick and overhead came his tail with a quick slap and hit with his stinger which was a half-inch long. You certainly wouldn't want this fellow in your slipper come morning.

I took the professor's picture. Shortly after that he had a bite and pulled out a small fish. While he was getting that off the hook I said good-bye and headed for the canoe. I figured he came out here to get away from people so my departure was probably not a big disappointment.

My camp that night was west of Terry in a sheep pasture. A giant cottonwood stood in the middle of the field and, like most sheep pastures, this one resembled a golf course. The aroma of sheep manure brought back warm memories of the farm. Dad had raised sheep as long as I could remember and that smell of sheep shit was so familiar.

There was dry wood everywhere. I gathered a pile for my fire and carried up some stones from the river to form my campfire.

My water system finally conked out. Renae had bought the water purifier for me and it was expensive, about 50 dollars. The filters were 35 dollars so I didn't bring any extra along. When I went in for supplies none of the sports stores carried them anyway. There was so much sediment in the Yellowstone from the high water that the filter just clogged up. I spent about 20 minutes trying to pump some water through. From now on I would have to get water from somewhere onshore.

I think my body muscles were slowly starting to feel better. The previous day was probably the high point of my discomfort. The Yellowstone forced a lot of effort out of me. Shoulders, lower back, butt – everything hurt. I would try to stand up and stretch when it was possible.

Probably one of the big reasons that I wasn't making more miles was because of the time I spent setting up my camp at night and repacking the next morning. Being able to enjoy this trip was having a nice camp at night. I also enjoyed putting together a tasty meal for supper. Along with some kind of meat I'd fix mashed potatoes, stuffing or noodles. After supper I'd wash a few clothes and hang them by the fire to dry.

This camp was one of the best yet. Sitting under that old sheep pasture cottonwood, I watched the fire for at least two hours. Even after I'd crawled into the tent, I continued to enjoy hearing the fire crackle. Its glow brought light to that side of the tent and made the inside less drab.

Up before light, I lit my gas stove to get water boiling for hot chocolate. Then unpacked the frying pan for my french toast.

Unfortunately by the time the dishes were washed and the tent packed it was almost 9 a.m. A lot of paddling time lost.

After three hours or so paddling, I'd pull over for 10 minutes and have some hot chocolate from my thermos. For lunch it was peanut butter or jelly sandwiches, a granola bar, apple and kool-aid. If I could, I'd eat and drift. If not, I'd pull up onshore.

Not far from Fallon I found an island that looked like a good place to camp. The wind was blowing pretty good so I pitched the tent on the leeward side. The sand on the island was like white powder.

The wind changed directions during the night and was really

howling. Finally I got up, opened the tent door and could see what looked like a sandstorm outside. There were clouds of white dust. I moved the canoe beside the tent door to help block the wind. Even though the cover was on, I turned it upside down. I shook out my sleeping bag and crawled back in. The wind still made the tent rattle like hell. Again I got up, moved some heavy driftwood over and tied the tent to that. It still shook all night.

In the morning the canoe was half buried in sand. That stuff was in my coffeepot, the food, everywhere. It took me two hours to clean up that mess. The wind didn't stop. When I took the tent down it got away from me, blowing across the island. If I hadn't grabbed it at the last minute it would have been in the river.

Glendive was a large city. I set up in a park there, then went in for water and supplies. I called home and finally got to talk to Dad; told him I was having the time of my life.

Later I again walked back into town for a couple beers. When I returned there was a young man sitting on a picnic table. He looked deep in thought, but I went over and introduced myself anyway. Soon I was hearing his life story.

Apparently this evening his girl stood him up and he came up here to think. When he was young, his father left home and his mother remarried a man the kids didn't like. When the family moved, he stayed here. He was big into the martial arts, but seemed like another high school graduate with no direction. I told him to save some money and go to college. Just what he needed, a lecture. I should lecture myself.

I wished the boy luck and headed for the tent. With the wind, there hadn't been much rest the previous night and I was bone tired.

About 15 miles past Glendive is the lower Yellowstone diversionary dam. Everybody said I'd need to go around it. I could hear the noise as I approached, so I glided the canoe over to the right edge of the river. The shoreline looked partly good until I stepped out and was immediately up to my thighs in muck. I finally got one leg back in the canoe and, using it and the canoe for leverage, I pulled the other leg free. Dangling each leg over the side, I did my best to wash them off. This all took about 10 to 15 minutes.

I let the canoe move down to where the large boulders forming the spillway started. It was Labor Day weekend so there were a half dozen tents and trailers in the clearing. The cooking grills were all out and some of the campers were fishing in a lagoon below the rocks. I tied the canoe tight against the rocks.

The fishermen were more than willing to help me guide the canoe down through the rocks. I left all the gear inside and closed the cover up tightly. With everything inside, the 16-1/2 foot Bell probably weighed 140 pounds. I had a coil of rope in my hand, which was attached to the canoe's stern. Moving from boulder to boulder, I would shout directions and keep the rope tight as they allowed it to follow the water flow through the rocks. Everything went well at first, but just prior to the lagoon they let it go early. With too much slack in the rope it crashed head on into a boulder before I could stop it. Some of the gel coat flew off, leaving a break in the Kevlar the size of a half dollar.

At the bottom I tied the canoe off and visited with the folks. Using my camera, a lady had been snapping some pictures as we worked the canoe through the rocks.

The folks invited me to join them for hamburgs and potato salad, but I didn't want to intrude, so I gracefully declined.

When I shoved off I got caught in an eddy and was soon sucked back into the lagoon. Four fishing lines were in the water there. I went over them, doing a nice job of tangling all four. The whole thing wasn't that impressive. I just wanted to get back in the river and leave the scene.

A mile down the river I pulled out and ate my peanut butter and jelly sandwich. I wished I'd taken up the hamburg, potato salad offer. It would have tasted much better than this.

A little water was starting to come in the canoe from the rock damage to the Kevlar. With some waterproof cement, I patched it up and had no more leakage.

There was an old abandoned road bridge that was fenced off. As I approached, I noticed an osprey circling about, then the nest on the top support caught my attention. After pulling up onshore I climbed the bridge structure for a closer inspection of the nest. The old bird did her best to divert my attention from the nest, but I got close enough to see three babies inside. I retreated back to the canoe, took a picture and left the mother and her family in peace.

It was fascinating to watch the osprey fish. When they spotted a fish, they would start out in this headfirst dive from a hundred feet up. Just before they hit the water they would have their talons out like spears. For a few seconds they would be underwater. When they surfaced, the osprey would tighten their grip on the fish, then lift off to the nest or some other place to devour the catch.

I was in North Dakota now. Up ahead were two towns, which on the map looked close to the river. It was Monday, September 1st, Labor Day. There would be about 10 more miles before the Yellowstone and Missouri Rivers joined.

It was late when I canoed to within view of the boat ramp south of the towns of Fairview and Cartwright.

Some days I really looked forward to socializing with humans again. On other days, it seemed like they violated the solitude of my journey.

There was a family camped by the boat landing. The parents were busy cooking on their grill while some little kids scampered about. Although there was a good campsite up river from them, I didn't want those kids messing with my stuff while I walked into town. I crossed the river and picked out another area that looked nice and sandy; however, I poked it with the paddle just to make sure it was solid.

For some reason, I was wearing the river sandals again when I stepped onto this nice sandy beach. Figuring the beach was solid, I had put my full weight down on that first step out. I immediately sank into white clay up to my knee. The sand was just a good camouflage for the white clay underneath. I was really stuck and the river sandal was doing a good job of creating some extra hold. With the other leg in the canoe, I couldn't get enough leverage to loosen the stuck leg. A piece of driftwood was within reach, so I positioned that so that I could put my unstuck foot on it to pull the other one out. When I attempted that, I slipped off the driftwood and now had both legs mired in the clay.

I'm trying to cuss quietly, but I'm sure my words carry across the river. The family on the other side is lined up watching me. Probably I'm providing better entertainment than their TV at home could offer.

The sandals acted like suction cups holding my feet in place. As much as I wiggled back and forth I couldn't get free. Finally I just started using my hands to dig around my legs until I moved enough clay to get my feet free. Mud was splattered all over me and all over the canoe when I got back in. The sandals went under the seat, never to be used again.

Back on the other side of the river I unloaded my stuff and washed all the clay off of my legs. It was almost dark. I hadn't begun to set my tent up yet. The folks came over and invited me to join in their picnic, but I was too proud and bullheaded. I had to do things my way. What I should have said was, "That sounds great, I'd sure like to join you," but instead I thanked them and said that when I got my tent set up I planned to walk into town for supper.

"Fairview is four or five miles away," they said.

"That's OK."

I blew up my air mattress, set up the tent and changed clothes. By the time I finished it was 9:30. Grabbing my water jug I started down the gravel road towards town. By the time I got there the restaurants would surely be closed. In a low voice I began to curse my stupidity.

Not too far down the road I met a car coming towards me. It slowed, then stopped right beside me. It was the nice family having the picnic next to me. Out the driver's side window the father handed me a bag with several fast food hamburgers in it and a Gatorade.

I was thoroughly stunned that someone that didn't even know me would drive ten miles just to get me something to eat. Especially after I had turned down their nice picnic offer.

"Gee, thanks. What do I owe you?" was my humble response.

"Nothing. We knew you were hungry. We could see you were having a bad day and felt sorry for you. Take the burgers and enjoy them. This is our good deed for the day." said the father.

I thanked him several times and said, "I won't forget your generosity. The next time I get a chance I'll pass this kindness along to someone else."

The mother leaned across, speaking through the father's window, "To be honest about it, the kids were the ones who suggested getting you something to eat. They kept asking us where you were going to eat and that you must be real hungry."

Moving to the rear window, I said, "Thanks, kids. You guys are great!"

The hamburgers tasted super. I was starved and in a very humble thoughtful mood. There was nothing wrong with doing things on your own, but there was also nothing wrong with accepting a little charity. If somebody is kind enough to offer something, I should learn to graciously accept. People offer because they think it's the right thing to do and they want to. They feel good to make you feel good. That exchange takes down barriers. When you refuse, you think you're doing them a favor, but you're really not.

My conscience started bothering me again, however, because those pesky little kids that I didn't want getting in my camp stuff were the ones who convinced their folks to get me something to eat. There was no way to rationalize my way out of that one.

The next morning I spent some time examining an old railroad drawbridge not far from my camp. It was really unique, for it was made for one man to be capable of raising it 50' to allow for river boats to pass. Building the bridge was a long and expensive undertaking. Through the use of several gears and counterweight one man could hand operate it. The top of the whole structure was almost 100 feet up. Of course I had to climb it to get a close look at the gears. On top, a strong gust of wind almost removed my trusty river hat, but fortunately a string held it to my neck.

As I surveyed this engineering marvel, I remembered what a fisherman had told me about the bridge. The gist of the story was that by the time the bridge was completed the railroads had completely taken over freight transportation from the river boats. This expensive bridge was raised and lowered only once.

From the bridge, the tracks ran through the only rail tunnel in North Dakota. The tunnel was over a quarter-mile long. I walked through it and was impressed with its size. It must have been around 15 feet high. The support beams were long 18-inch timbers placed two feet apart.

I continued my journey on the last few miles of the Yellowstone. Before long it would join the Missouri and disappear. The land was flatter here, the river quite docile. Its temperament was quite different from what it showed me in Billings. Now we would see what the Missouri would have to offer. I hoped that there would be some time to just relax, float along and enjoy the scenery. The Yellowstone hadn't allowed me to do that.

Top: Starting off on the Yellowstone.

Bottom: Another friendly train engineer waving.

Top: Osprey nest on top of bridge.

Bottom: The professor fishing near Powder River.

The Missouri – Lake Sakakawea

September 2nd to September 9th

There was no grand entrance to the Missouri River. The Yellowstone and Missouri meet to form Lake Sakakawea, which is the backwater from Garrison Dam. The dam lies well over 150 miles to the east.

At the point where the rivers merge, the river is only 100 yards wide. Soon it increases to about three-and-a-half miles. To the northeast I could see only water.

Sea gulls were flying overhead now. That was unusual, for I had seen none on the Yellowstone. The Yellowstone was muddy brown from the high water and now the water was clearer. As I entered the wider body of water, I thought there was a good chance I might be on the Missouri, but I wasn't sure. The vegetation along the shore was different too, as there were no cattails, just willows and brush.

I pulled close to a boat ramp where a man sat fishing and asked if this was the Missouri River. He probably thought I was a little nutty, but gave me a straight answer.

"Yep, this is the Missouri."

The wind was quite strong out of the southeast. The swells and waves coming off this lake were bothersome and something I wasn't used to handling. I tried to stay fairly close to the shoreline, but a mixture of willows and brush kept me further out than I wanted to be. There seemed to be little current, plus with the wind it was hard paddling. About a mile south of Williston, a bridge crosses an inlet. As I approached, I could see a fisherman underneath the bridge. Pulling up next to him, I introduced myself and asked how the fishing was going. It had been a bad day for him because of the constant wind. The fish weren't biting either, so he was doubly disgusted. I told him that I needed supplies and inquired how far away Williston was. Since he was having no luck fishing, he offered to drive me to town.

In Williston I refilled my water jug and picked up a few groceries. The fisherman was kind enough to wait outside, then drive me back to the river. Later, he left and returned with 10 packets of powdered eggs. I think that he was on government assistance with some extra subsidized food at home. The powdered eggs worked great for my breakfast french toast.

I removed my new food items from their original packages and put them in zip-lock bags. Then from a nearby gas station I called home.

Two boys came down to the bridge to fish, but the wind was blowing too much for them too. We did visit for awhile, and I wasted a lot of the day waiting for the wind to die down.

There were several more lakes formed by dams on the Missouri, so I was really starting to worry about how long this trip would take. My body was feeling good, but whether or not it would hold up with all the paddling I would have to do was the question. Neither did I have the faintest idea how many miles I could make per day. Would I ever make St. Louis by the last of October or would I have to have Dad pick me up short of my goal? We had talked about that possibility earlier, but it wasn't a pleasant thought.

My mood was rather low. The Missouri River was proving to be a disappointment. Certainly it would be a challenge to handle the wind and waves, but if this lake was an example of the backwater from the other dams on the river, it looked like a boring journey with lots of paddling. My idea of what the Missouri would be was what I saw near the expressway in Chamberlain, South Dakota.

I wasn't impressed with the scenery, either. It looked marshy and shallow along most of the shoreline. At least the water was pretty clear and there was certainly no shortage of it in any direction I could see.

Late in the afternoon I decided to leave, even though the wind was still howling. With everything packed up, I pushed out in the waves.

For 45 minutes I battled the open water with not much over a mile to show for my efforts. I decided to enter into the willows and use them for protection from the wind.

The willows were tall and rooted deep in the water. The waves crashed in so I stayed out in the middle of them. It was a cloudy day and once in the willows it was hard to see which direction I was going or even where the wind was coming from. My maps were just road maps, so there was no detail on the topography. It didn't matter though, because all I could see were willows anyway, even when standing up in the canoe.

I spent way too much time paddling in directions based on where I thought the wind was coming from. Finally I had to admit I was lost and fished around for my compass.

It was getting late. The willows didn't seem like an inviting place to spend the night, so I struck out a compass course to the east. That was a good decision, for in just a few minutes I was back out in open water.

When I finally found a place to go ashore it was dark. There was a 30-foot-high embankment there with rocks below. I needed to be careful going in. There was lots of driftwood around which I used with some small sticks to make a bed. I didn't even unpack the tent, just laid some blankets and my air mattress right on the sticks.

My bed felt pretty good, but then I was so tired just lying down on anything would have been a relief. The only distraction was the spiders that waltzed around on my face all night. I even found several in my sleeping bag the next morning.

The morning was pleasant with less wind. I lit my gas stove, put on my skillet and fixed up a half loaf of french toast. When that was polished off, I warmed water and made hot chocolate for my thermos. That would taste good with a granola bar for my morning snack. Not having to pack up the tent saved me plenty of time. Soon I was on my way. The marshy shoreline now changed to rolling hills, small cliffs and hardly any vegetation

A low pressure system had moved through, so the wind was behind me now. There might not be much current here, but at least the wind would be helping and not hindering my progress. Boldly I struck out for open water.

The wind slowly started to increase in velocity, probably up to 25 mph. Fortunately it remained at my back, and it was evident that I was putting some miles behind me. It was more of a problem keeping the canoe on course with the waves approaching from the rear. You couldn't see them coming, and they tended to shift the stern in one direction or the other.

Using the map, I tried to learn how to judge distance from points I could see. I would pick out a landmark 10 or 12 miles away and maintain whatever heading I needed to cover a straight line course towards it. When cutting across these large expanses of water, you needed to take into consideration wind, the direction of the waves and any current there might be. When I reached one goal, I would have to refigure everything for the next one, especially if the heading to it changed much.

Later in the afternoon the wind died down for awhile then picked back up even more that it was before. The swells alone were about four feet high. I came across some fishing boats that were seven feet or more in width. They were really getting thrown around and when I came close they were worried that their boats might get thrown into mine. The canoe was pretty stable. It was just riding up and down on the changing water surface. Most of the fishermen said they had enough and were heading in. They could not believe that someone would be out in the middle of this lake with a canoe.

As rough as this water was, I didn't feel frightened. My canoe cover was buttoned down and laced tightly around me. I had my life preserver on and I was gaining confidence in my ability to control my direction and progress. In fact, earlier in the day, before the wind picked up, I would attempt to surf on top of a swell for as long as I could. When I finally came down the canoe would skid. Once I almost lost it, so I quit doing that.

I spent the whole day out in that rough water and along toward sunset I spotted a lone fishing boat bobbing around some distance in front of me. I headed straight towards the boat. I thought the man would see me coming, but because the sun was directly behind me, he didn't. I was close enough to reach for his boat, but before I could touch it, a wave slapped the canoe lightly into his boat.

"Good afternoon. You must be one of those die-hard fishermen."

The poor guy was really startled. Regaining his composure, he said, "You must be one of those die-hard kayakers." He continued, "I wouldn't even consider having a canoe out here today." He examined his boat for scratches from my canoe.

"I was wondering if you might know of a good place to camp tonight," I said.

He told me that there was a fishing camp about four miles further down on the north shore. That's where he was staying.

I worked my way down the lake and spotted the camp he was talking about. Actually it was a big resort with lots of cottages and a small general store. As it was after Labor Day, the camp was about deserted.

There was a man in the office. He looked a little surprised when I walked in.

"I'm canoeing the Missouri. I need a hot shower and a place to pitch my tent. Also it would be nice if you had a washing machine for my laundry and a telephone I could call home on."

He smiled, then said, "You can pitch your tent in any of the campsites for seven dollars. The showers are out back. Sorry, no washing machine, but you're welcome to use the phone."

There were no other campers. I found a nice spot, got the tent set up and headed for the showers. Other than my cold river baths it was my first opportunity to stand under a shower and shave with hot water. Unfortunately I was out of clean clothes, so I picked out the cleanest of the dirties to put back on. Later that night, after the owner left, I washed all my clothes in the bathroom sink, then hung them out overnight to dry.

When I called home, I was able to actually talk to Mom and Dad; no answering machines this time. I told them everything I could think of about the trip. It had been a good 50-mile day and, with the shower and gaining confidence on the water, I was in really good spirits. Other than the machine messages, that was the first time they had heard from me. I told them that I had passed letters for them to fishermen to mail and that things were going really well.

The fisherman that told me about the camp finally came in with four nice walleyes. He said that this was really a good area for them.

I remarked that walleyes were a fish I hadn't eaten before.

While I was visiting with him, he laid the fish on a cleaning table and quickly filleted them out. When he was through, he handed me four nice fillets saying, "These are the cadillac of the fish world. Here you go; have some good eating."

From the cutting table to the frying pan; about as fresh as you could ask for. I rolled them in flour and cooked them in vegetable oil. With some stove top dressing, I had a real meal and ate all four fillets.

What a great day it had been, but judging from the low mood of yesterday I would have never guessed it would turn out so nice. Even with 50 miles of paddling through rough water my muscles felt good. Hearing the voices from home also gave me plenty of satisfaction. The rest of this trip might be OK after all. It still seemed like I was behind schedule. That cast a slightly gray cloud on my sunny attitude.

The next day was very nice with only a little wind at my back. The temperature had been in the 90's and was supposed to hit 100, so I decided it was time to just leisurely cruise along and try some sailing.

The sail was something I put together out of aluminum poles and a couple yards of nylon. It weighed around 6 lbs. On several occasions I tried to use the sail, but with each bend in the river the wind would be coming from a different direction. Sometimes it felt like it would blow me over. I didn't have enough hands to paddle into a wave and mess with the sail too. Once the sail was unrolled, it was difficult to roll it back up. For that reason, I stayed close to shore. Of course with the mast and guide wires up, the canoe cover was open, exposing the inside of the canoe and my gear to waves splashing in. I hoped that I hadn't carried this extra 6 pounds of sail all these miles for nothing.

Finally I got in a straight stretch of the lake and a five mph wind was at my back. I would try the sail one last time. The light breeze caught the unrolled sail and started giving me a nice little push. It was actually propelling me at a fairly good clip. It was working great. Now I could kick back and enjoy the cruise.

In the middle of a very remote countryside, I didn't feel that my modesty would be threatened, so I peeled off all my clothes and let the sun shine where it normally didn't. The sail stayed up for about six hours. It was the most pleasant and relaxing day I had experienced on the trip. There was, however, one drawback to having all this sunshine on parts of my body that weren't used to seeing the sun. And that was a very nice sunburn that caused tenderness and pain for several days. It made wearing underwear uncomfortable.

The stretch of Lake Sakakawea where I sailed ran through Fort Berthold Indian Reservation. The lake varied from 5 to 12 miles in width. I stayed right out in the center, because that's where it was smoothest. Closer to shore, in shallow water, there were waves. As long as the sail was working safely, there was no reason to stay close to shore.

I did spot some fishermen, so I put my clothes back on and passed over some letters to be mailed home. They seemed more than willing to help out. We visited about the weather, their fishing and my trip. That was the standard conversation whenever I ran across somebody to talk with.

About 7 p.m. I pulled up onshore, took my sail down and fixed a big dinner. The sunset was spectacular. While my water was boiling for supper, I took my camera and snapped a picture. It was so beautiful; like a scene out of a magazine. The whole western horizon was aglow with the sun's radiance. With my stomach full, I laid out on the blanket for an hour nap.

During all my hours of sailing that day, I only covered about 10 miles. The water was still very calm when I woke up, so I decided to canoe through the night to make up some distance.

It was an absolutely gorgeous evening. The water was smooth as glass and, although there was no moon, the stars seemed to light up the sky and were reflected off the water. It almost seemed that there were stars underneath the water.

I had heard coyotes before, but tonight their cries were especially clear. Occasionally fish would rise out of the water and startle me, but mostly it was the coyotes that filled the night air with sound. The owls would also blend in with their hoots and sometimes a nighthawk would come near. There were no man-made sounds or lights. No yard lights on the shore, no glow from a distant city, just light from an occasional shooting star. I was totally alone. This isolation gave me a mixture of new feelings. There are so few times in our life that we are not around other humans, or the noise they create, that absence of contact creates an empty feeling inside. The closeness of nature and its sounds did seem to fill the void and stir within me a deep appreciation of this unique opportunity to blend in.

For awhile I turned on my little radio and listened to music on some distant AM station. I quickly tired of that, shut it off and just leaned the canoe chair back on my gear and studied the stars. The night was so clear I could see satellites pass over. There was a light breeze now so it was a little chilly. I pulled the wool blankets up over my legs and was instantly in a cozy state. The stars reflected brightly in the water.

Early in the morning the sky clouded over and I started to paddle steadily to keep warm. The wind picked up and the waves increased from six inches to a foot in height. Even though I was paddling more, I couldn't seem to get warmed up.

Finally about 3 a.m. I was getting tired, along with being damned cold, so I decided to call it a night. The wind had picked up even more so the waves were up to two or three feet.

As I approached shore I could see that it looked rocky, but in reality these rock look-alikes were just clumps of clay formed by the waves. They were extremely slippery and the clay was hard to wash off my shoes.

My landing was a little rough, but I got the canoe out and found a grassy spot to put my air mattress on. The canoe gave me some protection from the wind. I put my light survival cover over the wool blanket and soon was warm and comfortable. I had been up since 8 a.m. the previous day, so my body was plenty tired.

At 5 a.m. I was awake. The noise from the waves whipped up by 30 mph winds was almost deafening. The wind was also carrying lots of sand. My blankets were also all covered with dew. I didn't unpack the tent, but I did remove some of my gear, which I moved up under an apple tree. The leaves were still on and it was far enough away from the shore to offer protection from both the wind and sand. With my bedroll repositioned, I again tried to get some sleep.

The wind blew all that day. It was much too rough for canoeing. I mended some holes in my blanket and tried to busy myself with chores, but mostly I laid around. Finally I decided to do some hunting and possibly find a farmhouse where I could get some water.

From a high point, I saw a house in the distance and walked a couple miles along a two track to get there. I thought it might not be appropriate to approach carrying a gun, so I hid it in the grass.

On the way back, I set my water down and shuffled through some brush to see if I could kick out some pheasants. Halfway through, a half-dozen birds flew out and I nailed one young rooster. I left that bird beside the water on the two track and went back to work my way through some more of the undergrowth. Another went up and I got him too. Now I had two nice birds for my cooking pot.

Back at camp I cleaned the birds and, with salt and onions, I simmered them for a couple of hours.

They provided a scrumptious meal and a welcome variation from duck, which I was growing tired of.

I was really getting uneasy about sitting around. Half a day had been wasted up at the Williston Bridge and here was another day about gone. The behind schedule worry was rearing its ugly head again. I had a great day sailing and watching the stars through the night, but not many miles were covered. There was a slight feeling of guilt that I should have been taking advantage of the smooth water to make time rather than just watching the scenery.

The radio weather report was calling for the wind to calm down after sunset. It was starting to get dark and I couldn't see much change. The waves reminded me of those I had seen in Washington State, where the Pacific Ocean crashes into the shoreline.

Since the start of this trip, I think that I had exercised good judgment in avoiding dangerous situations. Now I was about to deviate from that course of action and make a decision that was very stupid. Based on the light wind weather forecast, I considered pushing out in the lake and to make up lost time by paddling all night again.

Although I had confidence in my ability to handle waves in open water, these waves had been big enough to keep me off the lake all day. In fact, I had to move my stuff in 40 feet from shore just to avoid the spray when they came crashing in.

If I was going to do this I had to get through the breakers before dark. The sun was already setting. It was a panicky, dumb decision, but I decided to go. I wasn't sure what would happen and I was really scared.

Before I left I wanted to leave some kind of note in case something happened to me. In my notebook I gave a brief explanation of why I was doing this. I said that the winds had been 35 to 40 mph all day, but were supposed to be less tonight. I was behind time and didn't want to waste another day sitting around. Tomorrow might be as windy as today. I told Renae that I loved her and the same to my parents. The notebook went into one of my waterproof bags. I really would never want anybody to read this unless I drowned, but it did come from the heart.

I packed up everything and was ready to go; almost. Closing my eyes, I said a prayer asking for God's help to get me safely through this night. Reaching down, I picked up a small rock, rubbed it and put it in my pocket. This would be my lucky rock. I even made a wish on the first star I saw that night. I wanted everything going for me.

Using a sand bar as a push off point, I waited until the biggest wave of the day came crashing in, then paddled like hell before the next one. I wasn't fast enough, and the next one came crashing over the canoe, soaking me completely. Of course I had my life jacket on, but I had water up my nose, my hat was off and hanging, my hair was soaked. Still, I kept paddling as hard as I could to get out in open water away from shore.

The wind was behind me, still strong enough to cover me with spray from the waves. After the sun went down, it became very dark. A partial moon gave some definition to the waves. On my intended course they had been hitting the canoe from the 8 o'clock position (left rear), so I tried to keep the canoe in that same position when I paddled after dark.

The wind picked up even more. There was some hot chocolate in the thermos which would really taste good, but with the rough water I didn't know whether I could pour it or not. With one hand I held the thermos and with the other hand holding the flashlight, I tried to unscrew the cap. The canoe shifted unexpectedly with the next wave and the flashlight slipped from my hand, falling overboard. I watched for several seconds while my light sank lower and lower in the water. Some of this lake was supposed to be 200 feet deep. It really didn't matter though, 10 feet or 200 feet, my flashlight was gone. No more map reading for me tonight. There were a lot of channels and lagoons I could have made a mistake on. I knew eventually I would have to bear to the right (south), but I didn't know where.

It must have been around midnight when the moon disappeared. It was so dark now I couldn't see the waves. I could use the stars, but there was no horizon, no hills, no lights and of course no flashlight. The wind was picking up again. Waves were coming over the back of the canoe when they hit. I felt that I needed to keep paddling just for balance.

A light came into view ahead of me. It was clear out, so the light could be as much as 10 miles away. At least it gave me something to aim for. I wasn't sure how far I was from the Garrison hydro-electric dam. I had never been around one before and didn't know what to expect. Maybe the light was to mark the dam somehow. Which way I wasn't sure. What I did know was that I didn't want to be sucked down the intake into some generator.

With the light in sight, I did feel more confident. Now I wasn't floundering around out here going in some fruitless direction. Time to try the hot chocolate again. By feel I took off the top and poured some out. All I got was a half-cup. When I lost the flashlight I didn't get the lid back on tight. The rest had drained all over the inside of the canoe.

If I could figure where to land the canoe, I was ready to quit and get some sleep. Being out here was stupid. I was cold and my fingers were cracked and bleeding from constantly alternating between wet and dry. I paddled towards where I thought the shore was and must have been up in an arm of the lake, for the light disappeared. It seemed like I paddled a mile or so and was getting close to shore for I could hear the water smashing into the rocks. Without a flashlight, trying to find a suitable landing spot would be extremely hazardous. I decided it wasn't worth the risk. Turning around, I pointed the canoe directly into the waves. Soon I was back out of the cove with the light visible. As I got closer to the light, I could see that it was green and flashing. Maybe it was a channel marker, rather than something to do with the dam.

On the distant shore 5 to 6 miles to the left of the river light, I detected a floodlight. What a welcoming sight that was. If there was a residence, there probably was a boat dock. It would take quite awhile to cross the lake but I wanted to get my rear end on land.

As I approached the shore I didn't know what to expect. There appeared to be a quiet cove and sand bar ahead. Because of the wind, my lighter wouldn't stay lit, but as I flicked it, there was enough momentary light to get oriented to any obstruction I might encounter onshore. The landing was uneventful. I pulled the canoe onshore. What a relief it was to be on land after that ordeal. Physically and emotionally I was drained, but I was glad to be safe. Stepping out of the canoe, my legs were like rubber. When battling the waves, I had to lock my legs out straight against the sides to maintain a low center of gravity and for added stability.

There might be a nice place to camp up where the floodlight was. I walked in that direction. My feet were cold and clammy from having them in the water so long. Somewhere along the way the canoe had taken on quite a bit of water. As I walked toward the floodlight, I kept flicking my lighter to check the path. I didn't feel like tripping over anything tonight.

Approaching the floodlight, I could make out what looked like an old farmhouse with some big willow trees in the yard. The light made the willows look eerie as the wind shifted their limbs. A dark object was appearing in front of me. It was a wrought iron fence with a big gate at the end of my path. This place reminded me of a graveyard. I flicked my lighter. That exposed a no trespassing sign. There was something hanging from the gate that rattled with the wind. Another flick of the lighter and I could see what seemed to be a wind chime made out of animal bones. The skull of a dog or cat sat up on the gatepost. That was enough investigation for me. A more comfortable sleep could be attained down closer to the beach. I found a grassy spot, laid out my bedroll and passed out.

The next morning there was no wind, the sky was clear and the lake peaceful. I decided to make breakfast down at Garrison Dam. According to the map it was only 10 miles away. I didn't unpack the canoe, however I did dump out as much water as I could. It was nicely mixed with the hot chocolate that had leaked out of my thermos.

I stayed near the shoreline as I came closer to the dam. Still, I wasn't sure where the water intake for the generators was. It was time to be cautious again.

There was an older man on a dock fishing. I asked him where the best place to land the canoe would be. He told me of the boat ramp a half-mile back up river. We talked for awhile. He was a schoolteacher with the summer off and seemed interested in my trip.

I soon found the small cove where the boat ramp was located. The water was quiet, crystal clear and warm. It was time to clean this mess up, myself included.

Everything was covered with hot chocolate, even my sail. I pulled everything out on the dock, rinsed it off and laid it out to dry in the sun. Next I started washing clothes and hung them up to dry.

There was no one in the parking lot until the old pickup drove up. In it were two older ladies, maybe in their 70's. They spotted my laundry operation and came over to visit. When I told them about my trip they thought it was really neat. The ladies' husbands were fishing and they had just brought lunches down to them. They asked what my plans were that day. I told them that I would try to find someone to take my gear and canoe around the dam. The one lady said, "That's my husband's truck over there and I've got the keys. We would be happy to drive you. We'll be back in an hour."

It was time to do a little scrubbing on my body. I was pretty stinky. No one was around and the ladies wouldn't be back right away so I peeled down and grabbed a bar of soap.

I was out in the water when two more older ladies drove up. Apparently the two that would be giving me a ride told their friends. These gals just came down to say hello, too. Even though I was up to my chest in water I was still buck naked. I tried to be cordial, but I didn't go out of my way to lengthen the conversation.

By the time the women came back with the truck, I was about

packed. We loaded my stuff up and as we crossed the bridge they inquired if I needed groceries. I told them that I could use some, but hated to bother them. Nonsense, they would be happy to run me to the store. There were no other towns for awhile so I loaded up with groceries while the ladies waited in the truck.

While I was in the store I noticed some cherry cheesecake and willingly gave in to two pieces of that temptation.

Below the dam I graciously thanked the ladies for their kindness. I took their picture and they wished me luck. They left their address so I could let them know how my trip turned out.

The water temperature below the dam was very cold, probably in the high 40's. The fisherman that I talked to warned me about that. He said that water passing through the dam came from depths far below the lake's surface. Well that cold water made an excellent environment for rainbow trout and there were several fishermen on both sides of the river trying their luck to get one. As I passed by, everyone of them waved. I felt like a celebrity.

The Missouri now looked more like the river I expected when I started this trip. It was narrow, had a good current and I didn't have waves and swells to contend with. Because I was closer to the shoreline, I could see more wildlife and lots of geese.

I knew that I had around 180 miles before I ran into the backwater from the next dam, so for at least a few days life would be pleasant. I did wonder what it would be like after Bismarck, North Dakota. That stretch for 200 miles had been listed for experts only. We would see.

The Missouri – Lake Oahe

September 9th to September 20th

After Garrison dam I only went a few miles before setting up camp. A good share of the day had been spent cleaning up, getting around the dam, and shopping for supplies. I wanted to get a good night's rest and then strike out for Bismarck early in the morning.

Before sunrise I was on my way. The current carried me along at a good clip, but I set a steady pace paddling to assist the speed of the river.

The riverbanks were lush green, however, light from the rising sun highlighted a tinge of yellow in some of the tree leaves. A sure sign that fall was on its way.

Near Washburn I walked two miles for a sandwich, called home and left a message on the answering machines. From there it was about 35 miles to Bismarck.

I made good time until I was near Bismarck. The current started to slow. There were lots of cattails and a dense water plant I called duck grass. It was so thick that a duck could actually sit on it. And, there were thousands of ducks.

The duck grass was really hard to paddle through. Every time my paddle came out of the water there would be weeds attached. It was almost dark when I approached the residential section of Bismarck. I was tired. I decided that a dock would be just fine for my sleeping accommodations. Soon there was one in sight with no people around or boats attached.

With the canoe secured to the dock, I inflated my mattress, laid out the bedroll and settled for a light snack before bed. A couple of docks away from me there was this small group of men who seemed to be having a good time. Guess they were letting off a little steam after work. By the sound of their conversation they had probably consumed a few beers. They were aware of my presence, but didn't seem to care.

There were beaver around here. I had seen one earlier and either he or another one swam past the dock where the beer drinkers were sitting. One of the men spotted him. "There's a god-damned beaver!" Another said, "Why don't you go in and get your gun and shoot the S.O.B."

A man went into the house and came out with a rifle and flashlight, but they lost sight of the beaver. Disgusted, they decided to come down to my dock and see if I had seen him.

I was all ready for bed when these three dudes walked out on the dock with their gun and beamed a flashlight in my face. It was not my dock, but for the night it was my territory and these drunks were violating it without knocking. Nevertheless I tried to be civil.

"Ya seen any beaver swimmin' around down here?"

"No, I can't say that I have."

Of course that was a lie, but I didn't want this conversation or their presence to last any longer than necessary.

They shined the flashlight down on my canoe. The gun was evident in my gear. They asked a couple questions about my trip, but they were more interested in locating a beaver.

"If you see any beaver down here, shoot the bastards. We shoot them all the time because they chew the bark off my ornamental trees."

In a good-natured voice, I said, "Well, you know those beaver were here before you moved in. Why don't you put some fence around your trees?"

The guy with the gun responded, "Well, screw that. Why go to all that trouble when I can just shoot the damned beaver?"

The idea of just thoughtlessly killing beaver for a few ornamental trees kinda irked me.

Finally they headed back to their dock. The mosquitoes were really attacking me now so I got in my sleeping bag and pulled the blanket over my head.

I tried to fall off to sleep, but the beaver hunters kept at it. I'd hear one holler, "There's one there!" and a shot would ring out. There would be silence, then another shot. Finally a bullet went by close enough to get my attention. Whether it went over me at two feet or two hundred feet, there was no mistaking it was close, like a super-sonic bee. I poked my head out and their flashlight was pointed in my direction.

I'm not a profane person or one who goes out of his way to start a fight, but these boys had hit an untapped nerve in my body. I instantaneously came out of that sleeping bag and as loud as I could, I said, "Listen you motherfuckers. Put those guns away or a bullet is going to ricochet off the water and hit me. That last one was really close. I've come a long way and I have a long way to go. I don't want to end up shot in North Dakota."

My little speech was loud enough to wake any neighbor within a half-mile. There was a low murmur from the beaver hunters, then one said in a barely audible voice, "We'll put the guns away." That was the end of the shooting.

I left the dock before sunrise. Five or six miles down river I saw a road bridge ahead. There would be a remote stretch now and I needed groceries. After hiding the canoe, I walked a couple miles to a grocery store. It was open by the time I got there and, when I was through shopping, I had accumulated three big bags of groceries. That was more of a load than I could comfortably haul back to the bridge. Foreseeing my problem in advance, I struck up a warm con-versation with some of the other customers standing in line and soon I had a willing volunteer to drive me back to the river.

Back on the river there was a strong head wind. I really busted my ass paddling but was not showing much progress. I hugged the shoreline and finally found a small cove to pull into. The radio weather forecaster said it would be windy all day.

In the distance I could see a lagoon with what looked like a pub-lic boat ramp. The closest town on the map was Huff. Something was going on here, for about 20 boats were lined up on the shore. Other boats were out in the river darting back and forth. I hadn't filled my water jugs yet, plus it was lunch time. With the wind, I wasn't making much progress either. I might just as well look for a place to camp.

At the boat ramp I talked with two elderly gentlemen who told me that all the boat activity was associated with a national bass fishing tournament. They were the judges. They explained how the tournament worked and showed me the prizes. First prize was $25,000 cash plus a new Dodge truck. There were other nice prizes which included boats and fishing gear.

Lots of brand new trucks and boat trailers were lined up with stickers and decals on them, advertising various fishing-related equipment. I had seen all this on the TNN TV network and here I was right in the middle of it.

The judges explained to me the rules. Each fisherman has a daily limit for three days and I believe the winner has the highest average of six fish. The rules seemed pretty strict. They even had an overseer for each boat to prevent cheating.

The men were very interested in my trip so I gave them a rundown of where I'd been and my destination. They pointed to an old hand water pump when I asked about filling my water containers. The water was real sulfury as it had been about everywhere. I don't know how folks stand it, but nobody complains. Mixing it with kool-aid helps to kill the taste.

After eating lunch I asked about a campsite. I was told that this campground was full, but there was another a half-mile down river that should have spaces available.

The campground they were talking about was nice and rustic. Also I found it empty, so I had the whole place to myself. In the west there were a lot of dark clouds, and even though it was only 1 p.m. I decided to put up the tent and stay for the rest of the day.

I had a duck from an earlier hunt in a plastic bag. I started simmering it with onions and peppers. Meanwhile I sat at a picnic table and wrote some letters. There was a long one to John Veneklasen and as my hand tired, shorter ones to other folks at home I hadn't talked with on the phone. At 7 p.m. it started to rain for a couple hours. The pitter-patter on the tent finally put me to sleep.

There was a light rain in the morning. After a big pancake

breakfast I packed up. I wasn't in any big rush, just took my time getting started.

This was Lake Oahe, another large lake formed by a dam on the Missouri. This lake was the largest I would encounter, about 200 miles from Bismarck to the Oahe Dam and the one the planning book said was recommended for experts only. From what I could see it wasn't any different than Lake Sakakawea. Just a lake that the wind could use to whip up some nice waves and swells.

People told me that these lakes were as much as 10 feet higher than normal. This presented a different kind of problem. The waves being around four feet high, I tried to stay reasonably close to shore. The higher water level covered stumps and logs that were normally not submerged. It was difficult to see them as the canoe did its up-and-down number in the rough water. Sometimes I wouldn't see them until the last second.

The waves were behind me now. I thought I was making good progress threading my way between the stumps when a large wave lifted the entire canoe out of the water. Just as suddenly, the wave deposited me back down on the top of a stump and the canoe started to roll off on its side. Pushing down hard on the left kept the canoe from turning all the way over, but my whole left side got soaked. I decided it would be safer to be in the open water and avoid these dangerous hidden obstacles.

Everyone I talked to told me to avoid the Indian towns at night. In daylight it would be safe enough, but no telling what would happen at night. My next stop would be Fort Yates which was on an Indian reservation. I needed some radio batteries, film and a flash-light, so my plan was to get close to Fort Yates tonight, then go in early in the morning for what I needed.

With the wind behind me, I was making good mileage and should be getting close to Yates. It was totally dark out now, but there was a light in the sky on the western side of the lake. That must be Fort Yates. Where I crossed over to the west side the lake must be around four miles wide. Logs had washed up on the shore and I could hear the water hitting the log piles. There was a little bay between the logs where I smoothly brought the canoe in.

It was really a pretty night out. A grass embankment was in front of me and some higher ground beyond that. I decided to strike out and look for the town. According to the map it should be about two miles from the river. Away from the river the grass was knee-high, like an unused pasture. Making my way to the top of the hill, I found a two track road. The road wound around the small hills and I figured it would join a gravel road that might lead to the town. Instead it ran into a cedar grove which was very dark inside. Uncomfortably dark. I decided to leave that road and go directly to the highest hill I could see. It took awhile, but I reached the top and on the other side was a farm with bright-looking fluorescent lights. It was not Fort Yates.

The fact that Fort Yates must be some distance away really didn't disappoint me. It was such a beautiful, pleasant night, I just laid down on my back in the tall grass and watched the stars. Probably I laid there for a half-hour just reflecting on my river experiences both good and bad. Each day offered something different, something unexpected. I wasn't looking for dangerous situations; they just seemed to happen randomly, and I reacted through instinct the best I could. I'm sure Lewis and Clark with all the rest of the pioneers had to do the same thing in a lot more hazardous conditions. Anyway, I was really enjoying this trip and before I left the top of that hill I closed my eyes and thanked God for this experience. I also asked for him to keep watching over me all the way to St. Louis.

That night I didn't set up the tent because there were some prickly pear plants close by that might puncture it. I didn't even inflate my mattress, just rolled a tarp out on the soft prairie grass by the canoe. It was soothing to hear the waves splash against the logs. I laid on my bedroll and covered with my foil-lined emergency blanket. My head was out of the covers all night and the next morning my hair was soaked with a heavy dew. It's a wonder I didn't catch cold.

As it got light out I could see by the map that Fort Yates was still 10 miles away. That would take me about an hour and a half. I passed a nice fishing boat that the owner was having a problem getting started. He was bobbing around in the waves and I could tell that within short order the boat's battery would be dead if he kept it up.

Further on I saw another boat which I paddled over to. I told those men about the guy aways back that couldn't get his motor started. His battery was probably dead by now and perhaps a couple of bucks could be made towing him. They said there was no public river access to Fort Yates, but told me the direction to go for the grocery store.

When I first approached the shore there were a couple of kids playing nearby, but they soon disappeared. I dragged the canoe up between some boulders and a logjam and tied it off.

I wanted to keep a low profile here. I looked around and couldn't see anyone.

I walked about four blocks into town. There was an ambulance sitting on one side of the street with one of the paramedics, a heavy guy, nearby. I asked him for directions to the store. For some reason, there was this persistent feeling inside that my canoe wasn't safe. It took me only five minutes to walk back where the canoe was. The tarp had been pulled up by someone. Taking inventory I found my radio, headphones and a new flashlight missing. That really pissed me off. The radio wasn't that expensive, it's just that I would miss the news and weather forecasts. I could usually only pick up one AM station but it helped when there was boredom. If I had been gone longer than five minutes I probably would have really been cleaned out.

About a half-mile down the river I came ashore again. This time I pulled the canoe up in the brush and camouflaged it with tree branches. From there I climbed up a hill and around a board fence behind the stores.

First I stopped by the gas station and filled the fuel bottle. The lady was nice. She said she would keep an eye on the bottle while I was in the grocery store.

Around the corner from the grocery store was a boarded up church. On the church steps sat five Indians. They looked like they were 35 to 40 years old and what a nasty looking bunch they were. They all had huge noses that looked deformed with big black spots on them. The noses were about three-quarters the size of a tennis ball, with dimples, red blisters and peeling. Maybe they were afflicted with skin cancer or something, but it was obvious they never used sun screen.

Well here I come in my white-man clothes, so obviously I had money. They looked at each other to see whose turn it would be to hit me up for some cash. Finally two got up at the same time, but one sat back down. The one standing motioned me over. "Ya got some change for me to get something to eat, or 25 cents for a pack of cigarettes?"

I gave him a dollar bill. He seemed happy with that.

When I entered the store everyone started staring at me. I was the only white person in the store and it was like they had never seen one before. I didn't think too much about it, just went about picking up the items I needed. The flashlights were eight to ten dollars, too expensive. I could hold off on that.

The Indian from the church steps came in after I did. He was lingering around the meat case, then I saw him carefully slip a package of cold meat in his pocket.

I stood in the grocery line for several minutes. There were some old folks and kids in line too; they were giving me the once-over again.

With two small bags I headed out of the grocery store, back toward the gas station to get my gas. The Indian apparently had left the store ahead of me. He sat with his buddies on the steps.

As I approached he walked towards me with the package of cold meat in his hand. "Mister you want to buy some cold meat? It's still nice and cold. Give me two dollars." The meat was sliced beef kidney or something. I just said, "No." But, what I wanted to say was, "You took my money in that store just to shoplift. If you hadn't had a buck for cigarettes they probably wouldn't have even let you in."

After picking up my fuel bottle I ducked behind the store and hurried through the woods down the hill to my canoe, looking behind me regularly. I thought there was a reasonable chance that someone would be there and try to roll me. At the canoe I wolfed down some cookies and drank a quart of chocolate milk. I felt like I was being watched.

I packed the canoe quickly and was on my way. What a hole this place was. The houses had looked all run-down with broken windows and cars jacked up in the front yard with no tires. There were several men just sitting around drinking beer. There was a lot of poverty here, obviously, but why did the place have to look like such a dump. At least I knew why it was wise to stay out of these towns after dark.

A few miles down river, just before the South Dakota border, I spotted a fishing camp. Up onshore there were a bunch of young guys my age who had returned from quail hunting. They just finished loading the dogs in the back of the pickups and now they were putting supplies on a pontoon boat for a night of fishing. They had coolers full of beer and a grill. It was Friday and they were unwinding with an afternoon of hunting and an evening of fishing and beer drinking.

There was a snack bar and grill close by plus a laundromat. After ordering a couple of hamburgers, I put my dirty clothes in the coin laundry machine and bought a flashlight with batteries in the small store. With the laundry going, I crossed back over to the snack bar for my hamburgers. There were a couple of cute girls working the grill and I told them all about my trip as I ate my burgers. The flashlight I bought didn't work, so when I picked up my laundry, I returned the light and got my money back.

When I called home it was about 3 p.m., and I guessed nobody would be in at home. That was the case, but I left messages on the answering machines anyway.

Back at the canoe I packed away my clean clothes and enjoyed a beautiful sunset. I would travel tonight and try to make up some time.

At dusk I shoved off and there was a 15 mph breeze at my back. Not long after that the wind shifted around into my face and picked up some. The waves were three feet high now. It was hard paddling. The surface water seemed to be holding me back.

There was no moon, but I could see a yard light on the eastern shore several miles ahead. The lake was about two miles wide here so I angled across towards the light. Not much progress was going to be made tonight, but if I could put an extra 10 miles behind me that would help.

All of a sudden, close to where I was headed, I could see flares going off. That happened for at least an hour before I reached the other side. Closer to shore there seemed to be more floodlights and vehicles skirting around. It must be some sort of military exercise. There were some hills close to shore that blocked the wind and allowed the water to be calm. The flares stopped, but there was some kind of movement on shore. I could imagine there were military guys out there on night maneuvers. They probably had night vision goggles and were watching me approach.

There were some dark objects onshore. The objects seemed to move around some, then stop. At about 50 yards out I decided to let them know that I wasn't part of their exercise.

"I see you guys sitting up in the weeds. I'm just passing through in my canoe. I'm not part of your exercise. I'm not the enemy."

There was no movement from the objects so I paddled right towards them. We'd make these guys do something, commit themselves some way. Suddenly they took off and ran up the hill. Hell, it was two mule deer. My mind must have been playing tricks with me. Still it was a tense few minutes and my heart was really pumping.

After I calmed down, I brought the canoe up onshore, threw my bedroll on some driftwood and was soon asleep.

When the sun came up I got a close look at my surroundings and I discovered that I was right in somebody's neighborhood. There were several houses there with a good view of my little nest from their living room window. No one seemed to care that I was there so I proceeded to cook up a nice bunch of french toast. While I was cooking I thought, what in the world had I seen the night before? What were all the flares and vehicles running around? Was it a figment of my imagination or was there some type of exercise going on in the distance?

Renae had sent a New Testament with me. I never had read the bible much before, but after breakfast I sat back and read about 30 pages.

The water was calm here. At 10 a.m. I left the cove for open water and there was lots of wind, right in my face. Mobridge was 30 miles away and it would be an all-day project getting there. The wind would cut my speed in half.

Not far from Mobridge there was a good-sized highway bridge crossing the river. There was a large fishing boat bobbing around in the four-foot-high waves. It must have been a charter fishing vessel, because the crew wore uniforms.

When I was within shouting distance one of the crew hollered,

"What the hell you doing out here in a canoe?" Approaching close enough to be heard, I told them where I was from and where I was going. One gentleman on board owned a marina close by. He pointed in that direction. "Paddle over there and I'll set you up with a place to camp tonight."

"Thanks anyway," I told him. "I'm going to go down to Mobridge and camp. Need to do some shopping."

Just past the bridge I pulled up and stepped out. It was two inches of water and six inches of muck. I hid the canoe in the weeds and secured it to a log.

The walk to the store was about three-quarters of a mile. At a department store I purchased a small map light type flashlight, some shotgun shells and called Mom.

Outside of the store I sat on the sidewalk enjoying my chocolate milk and cookies. I didn't think much about it before, but guess I looked a lot different than most folks along the river. By now I was pretty well tanned. My long hair was bleached almost blond from the sun and hung out from under my river hat which I wore all the time. Probably I just looked out of place, for a couple of old ladies came up asking where I was from. After relating my standard story line they wished me lots of luck and said good-bye. Before leaving they said, "Be careful. There's a storm coming."

Southwest of town there was this huge black cloud heading in this direction. My 10-minute walk turned into a short run back to the canoe.

There was a lot of brush around, most of it about four feet tall. An unused looking two track was close, so I quickly set up my tent in the middle of the road. I wanted to have some place to get under-cover before this storm hit. By now there were some wind gusts from the storm with lots of lightning.

It was probably a combination of all the rushing around and my nerves, but I had this intense need for a bowel movement. If I could just hold off until the storm passed. Unfortunately there was no holding to this intense urge. It was now a dire need. As the storm came closer and the lightning flashed, I grabbed a roll of toilet paper and looked for a convenient place to do my duty. I sure didn't relish baring myself in the rough-looking brush. Probably some rattle-snake was just waiting in there to bite me in the ass. This road looked remote enough, I would take the easy way out.

Stepping off a respectable distance from the tent, I lowered my pants and assumed a hunter's crouch. What a disgusting moment this was. All the work putting up the tent to avoid the storm and now I would be drenched out here with my pants down.

In the distance I could hear the noise of an engine. At first I didn't think much about it. I was too engrossed in what I was doing and worrying about the storm. The engine noise grew louder. It became apparent that someone was barreling down this two track in an ATV (all terrain vehicle). My tent was set up close to a sharp turn in the road. If the dude coming down the road wasn't alert, he could plow right into my tent after turning the corner.

Not only did I have the thunderstorm to worry about, now there was this speedster coming. At least part of my job was done so I hurriedly pulled up my pants and knelt down out of sight behind the tent.

The driver of the ATV slowed coming around the corner. This action probably saved the tent, because after the turn I could hear him locking up his brakes as the tent caught his attention. He was there for a few minutes, occasionally revving up his engine. Probably he was also catching his breath from the near collision with my tent. Finally he turned his machine around and left.

The thunderstorm narrowly missed my campsite. There were just a few sprinkles and no more follow-up storms. It had all been a period of high stress for me though. Just another one of those surprise encounters canoeing the Missouri. I wondered how many more there would be. The more I thought about it though, the funnier the whole thing seemed. It was certainly worth a few chuckles.

A tough head wind shortened another day. At 1 p.m. I called it quits. I decided to go hunting, but first I set up the tent and piled up a large pile of driftwood for my evening campfire.

A couple of ducks went up but I missed. I'd really rather have a pheasant anyway, so I left the river in search of some pheasant cover. There was a large cow pasture nearby which looked promising. In the distance I could see three or four cattle, but in this end of the pasture there were some thick weeds. I stepped through the barbed wire and started making some passes through the tall stuff. Some birds flew out one at a time and I nailed a nice pheasant.

I think the cattle had noticed me before, but the gunshot heightened their curiosity. They were coming in my direction. After a few minutes, I found my dead pheasant, just in time to see three long-horned bulls heading towards me at a very fast pace. With my gun and game I gingerly slipped through the barbed wire fence. The bulls stopped 100 feet away and their snorts sounded very close. They seemed to be satisfied that they had rid their pasture of this stranger. I was happy to have noticed them before they came any closer.

I made a big campfire that night. Even though I went to bed early, I still enjoyed the fire crackling outside and the shadows it created on the tent. Later in the evening the wind picked up, rattling the tent all night. Once I got up to secure part of it to some driftwood. The night before, the campfire provided enough light to see spiders all over the beach. The next morning when I turned over my canoe, it was full of them.

Highway 212 is a major road that crosses the Missouri heading west into a large Indian reservation. The sunset was so spectacular that I left the canoe onshore and climbed up on the bridge to take pictures. There were some fishermen near the bridge that I struck up a conversation with. They said there was a small fishing village east that had a good restaurant and bar. That really sounded good. More and more I was looking forward to a restaurant meal.

I put up the tent, grabbed my water jugs, and set out for the restaurant. The evening was pleasant with a light breeze. It seemed good to be out of the canoe and stretch my legs.

The entrance to the restaurant was near the bar. I asked the lady behind the bar if I could get my water jugs filled before I left. She said she would be happy to fill them up, that I should just leave them by the door. They'd be ready for me when I finished eating.

Once again I could sense the eyes of the other patrons on me as I picked out a nearby table and sat down. They seemed to be friendly eyes, probably just curious who the stranger was.

The waitress was soon at my table with her ordering pad. After a

quick glance at the menu I said, "I'm really starved. I've been paddling my canoe all day on the way to St. Louis. I'd like some chick-
en and how about some extra mashed potatoes."

"That's no problem. We'll get you filled up, don't worry,"
she responded.

While the food was being prepared I slipped to a barstool for a
beer. When the waitress came out with my chicken, she also had a
separate plate with about three servings of mashed potatoes and
gravy on it. While she was setting down my order she inquired more
about my trip. The folks at the next table were now tuned in.
Between forkfuls of mashed potatoes and bites of chicken I had to
answer questions. Certainly I appreciated everyone's interest, but
the conversation sure cut into the enjoyment of my meal. It didn't
end there. I was invited up to the bar and the conversation went on
as the beer went down.

Finally I said good night to everyone, left the waitress a generous
tip, picked up my water jugs, an extra beer and headed back for a
nice sleep. I was really in a relaxed mellow mood with a full stomach. My spirits quickly changed when halfway down the hill I could
see my tent was missing. The wind was howling now. A hundred
feet across the parking lot was the tent all collapsed in a patch of cattails. My gear, clothes, cookstove, everything was rolled up as a ball
in the tent. There was over 100 pounds of stuff inside, otherwise the
tent would probably have blown away. I struggled to remove the
gear from inside and in the process kicked over the half-full beer
that I had brought back with me. That pissed me off. The more gear
I took out, the lighter the tent was, which made it even more vulnerable to the wind. I put the tent over my head and walked back
across the parking lot. I was a little tipsy from all the beer, but the
struggle with the tent didn't rile me up as much as the spilled beer.

After wrestling the tent around for sometime, I had it solidly tied
down again and proceeded to carry back all my gear. Moments after
crawling in my sleeping bag I was asleep.

In the morning I was back up at the same restaurant looking for
a big breakfast. A closed sign hung on the door. It was the tail end
of fishing season so their open hours were limited. I had to settle for

two pop tarts.

I made good time for about 30 miles then the river made a big bend towards the northwest for 10 miles. That put me right back facing the wind. I didn't want to fight the waves any longer, so I fixed a nice dinner of pheasant and set up my camp. It was a perfect-looking camp arrangement. I was so proud of it that I took a picture, then later made a drawing for a letter to Grandma Bernice.

My map indicated that I was on a narrow peninsula. The river went northwest for 10 miles then swung back around the peninsula heading southeast for an equal distance. After that the flow was pretty much due south for 30 miles to Oahe Dam.

With some hot chocolate I relaxed and wrote a couple of letters. My back was a little sore from all the paddling that day, but still I felt good. There was a full harvest moon out, and I remembered that I had told Renae that the night of the full moon we would watch it from different parts of the country, but might feel a little closer with its presence. She was home now after a nice tour of the western states with Shelby.

It was a warm evening. I planned to just lie on top of my sleeping bag. Before lying down I looked out the tent window and there in the moonlight I could see several raccoons heading toward the canoe. What they wanted was to get into my food sacks. When I came out of the tent they scurried up the hill. To be on the safe side, I brought the food into the tent. Not far behind the tent was a frog pond. I went to sleep with their continuous croaking.

The morning brought a lot of cackling from roosters up in the hills. I would take it easy, hunt for awhile, then paddle down to Oahe Dam.

I took five shotgun shells and headed up into the hills. These were green rolling hills with a foot-and-a-half of underbrush. First I kicked out a mule deer, then an antelope sprang out in front of me. The pheasants were in the ravines and they would run ahead and not fly until they reached the top of the hill. It was hard work trying to roust them out, and each time they flew there were only a few seconds before they were out of sight. I kicked out 5 birds and shot five times with nothing to show for the effort.

At a high point I could see the river circling back down on the other side of the peninsula. I debated whether to spend two hours hauling my stuff over the half-mile to the other side or canoe around. I made the mistake of canoeing around. That took 3 hours and a lot of wave battling to get back to that point directly opposite my camp on the other side.

It was late in the day and I still hadn't arrived at the dam. Finally I saw some fishermen.

Earlier I had found a brand new fishing lure, so as I approached their boat, I greeted them and said, "Hey I've got something for you!"

I bent down and rummaged around under the seat for the lure. When I came up I could see an apprehensive look in their eyes, like maybe I had been reaching for a gun.

They were more than happy to have the new lure and directed me to a boat landing about five miles farther down near the dam. Those fishermen were from North Dakota, down here on a week's vacation, trying different fishing spots each day. They said the dam was well-lighted and that I would easily see it in a mile or so.

About 9 p.m. I found the boat ramp. When I arrived, there was an old guy and his wife pulling out a bass boat. An old pickup truck with a camper on it was parked near with a trailer for the boat.

The old folks were from Minnesota. They came down every year to fish. I told them my story and said I was looking for a ride around the dam. They said they were sorry but couldn't help me out. Oh well, there were several other people out fishing with four or five trucks and trailers still parked there.

It was forecast to be quite cold tonight, so I didn't expect that the rest of the fishermen would be out all night. They started coming in one boat after the other. To each party I introduced myself. They all had some excuse not to help me out. It was getting late and cold. There was one truck left in the lot. That truck didn't have a trailer attached, so maybe I would have better luck. I hoped so, because it would be my last shot tonight.

There was a full moon again tonight, which brought the last fishing boat into view while they were quite far out. It was damn cold out now and I had both a sweatshirt and jacket on. Approaching the dock, they idled down the engine and I was right there to welcome them.

"I sure hope one of you guys owns that white pickup truck up there."

As soon as they hopped out I introduced myself and said I was looking for a ride to portage the dam.

One guy came closer and responded, "Well, Scott Galloway, who's canoeing down the Missouri and looking for a ride to portage around the dam ... Yes, no problem, you want a beer?"

With four men to lift it, we could put the loaded canoe right in the back of the truck without me having to unload it. The other two guys left with the boat in another pickup I hadn't noticed.

It was about a four-mile drive around the dam. My benefactor was a lawyer on the third day of a fishing trip. He seemed like a real nice fellow. He told me about the guy that owned the restaurant, boat ramp and campground below the dam. There was some excellent fishing there, so the guy did a good business.

We unloaded my gear in a grassy spot underneath the yard light by the boat ramp. The other two fishing buddies showed up and they invited me into the bar with them.

The owner of the place was in his 30's and the fishermen seemed to be old friends with him. I was introduced.

I didn't buy a beer that evening, but I did drink several. They were all complimentary. The topic of discussion that evening was the other people that had canoed the Missouri. There didn't seem to be many, but a couple were quite noteworthy.

Once a lady came down in some sort of inflatable canoe. I'm not sure where she started from, but was terribly sunburned. They said she spent most of her daytime hours under a tarp.

Then there was Victor. He was 58 years old and had started at the headwaters as I had. Victor was about out of money. He also was very concerned about his body weight loss. The owner let him stay in a cabin free for two days and kept him stuffed with pancakes to put some weight back on. Victor had sent a post card that he made it OK. Those guys seemed to have a lot of funny stories about Victor.

At 1 a.m. I said good-bye and left the bar. With several beers on an empty stomach I was certainly feeling no pain. The wind had picked up, so with much difficulty I finally got the tent up and went to bed. It was supposed to be cold that night so I covered up with everything I had.

It wasn't a very good night's sleep. The yard light lit up my tent, plus there were a lot of people loading and unloading fishing boats all night.

The morning brought a light rain with some fog. In the restaurant, I had a big pancake breakfast and thanked the owner for letting me camp there.

The water below the dam was very cold. When I pulled out of the lagoon by the boat ramp, I tried to be real careful entering the fast water. I sure didn't want to turn over and freeze my rear end in that stuff.

There still were several fishermen around. I visited with a couple and waved at the rest.

The current was about 7 mph so I should reach Pierre in a half-hour. After each dam it seemed like I was starting a new part of the trip, and again I was looking forward to what this new stretch of the Missouri had in store for me.

Top: Myrtle Liebing (right) drove me around Garrison Dam with her friend Luella Matzke.

Bottom: All cleaned up at Garrison Dam.

Top: Camp by frog pond on peninsula before Oahe Dam.

Bottom: Camp on Lake Sakakawea.

Halfway

September 20th to September 26th

Pierre would be a definite stop for water and groceries. The next city would be Chamberlain, South Dakota, which would be about 80 miles away.

On the outskirts of Pierre I located the boat ramp, but the fast current kept pushing me by it as I tried to land. I paddled back upstream for the second time and on the next pass was able to bring the canoe in.

After asking for directions I walked a little over a mile through town to the grocery store. I probably bought more than I needed, and ended up with two heavy bags to carry back.

There were some security guards standing in line with potato chips and beer. It looked like they were planning a little party. I started visiting with them, and in the course of the conversation, I mentioned that I was on my way canoeing from Billings to St. Louis. Everyone close in my checkout lane turned to listen to the conversation and there were questions coming from the lane beside us. I was kinda embarrassed. After that I learned to keep my mouth shut in public. I enjoyed telling people about my trip and appreciated their interest, but I didn't want people to think I was just trying to get attention.

Anyway, the security guards were impressed with what I was doing so I got a ride back to the river in a new Blazer. They were interested in looking at my canoe and gear. Someone asked if I could stay for a few extra minutes. They wanted to get a newspaper reporter down here. I said I'd wait for a half-hour.

Within 30 minutes I had things packed up. I waited another 15 minutes then decided to leave. I really didn't feel like talking to a reporter anyway. It was about 9:30 a.m. The current gave me excellent speed so I could paddle at my leisure and enjoy the scenery.

The river outside of Pierre runs straight southeast for 25 miles. On one side there were some very high limestone cliffs, maybe 100 to 200 feet high. On the other side it was quite marshy.

This was a remote stretch of river. Once more I stripped down to my birthday suit and was working on a total body absorption of sun.

I was becoming pretty good at estimating water current speeds. Using specific points I could identify on the map, I could estimate my arrival times, within 15 minutes. Even without referring to the map, I could also now judge quite accurately how far away prominent landmarks were.

On the ridge of a cliff I saw a raccoon. That whole scene looked attractive for a picture so I pulled the canoe to the bottom of a ravine where cattle had been coming to drink. Out of the canoe, I was up to my thighs in mud. It was quite an effort to get the canoe out, but finally, with camera in hand, I made my way through the pine trees. No shoes, sox or clothes, there I stood on the top of the cliff exposed to the world. Ha. I took a picture in each direction down the river. Certainly it was a beautiful setting, but I doubted if the camera could adequately capture even part of it.

It seemed like the Oahe Dam allowed less water to pass because the water level seemed much lower here. After 50 miles the current started to slow too.

The country I was passing through now was the Lower Brule Indian Reservation. There was a town associated with the reservation located not far away from the Big Bend Dam. My plan was to camp outside of town that night, then find someone to help me portage around the dam the next morning.

It was Saturday evening. There seemed to be several weekend fishermen out along the shoreline. One man had his three sons with him. They looked like they were 10 to 13 years old. Everyone had lots of questions. "Where ya headed? Where you been? Where ya from?" One group asked if I was hungry, then tossed out some apples. I caught one and retrieved the rest from the water.

I ended up paddling until almost 10 p.m. The glow of the lights from the Indian town were evident. I could see their water tower and yard lights, but I couldn't find a suitable place to land. With the water level down it was like a mud flats. A few times I tried to push in to shore, but each time I got the canoe stuck in the mud and had to back paddle out.

Finally, almost past the town, the water was deep enough to reach shore. I climbed over an embankment and found a nice park. I was a little uneasy camping this close to town on Saturday night. People had told me plenty of stories and issued warnings about Saturday nights in these Indian towns. Government checks were being cashed and there would be lots of drinking and a hell of a time had by all. I didn't want anybody messing with me or my gear that night. I kept my gun loaded and handy.

Early the next morning I walked into town for breakfast. It was a small town with a couple of casinos. Things weren't opened up yet, however, the cook at the restaurant said she'd open up early for me.

After a nice breakfast I asked a security lady if she knew of someone who could help me portage around Big Bend Dam. She said she couldn't leave her job but maybe she could call a friend.

The restaurant was officially open now. There was a line of people waiting to come in. One couple, in their 40's, looked like nice folks. I introduced myself, told them what I was doing and asked if perhaps they could drive me around the dam when they finished breakfast.

"Sure. We'd be glad to help out," they said. And, they were ready to do it before eating breakfast.

Even though the dam was only a half-mile away, to get below the dam was 20 miles by road. This turned out to be a big deal favor and I felt guilty for them leaving the breakfast line to do it.

The couple were on an all-expense-paid hunting expedition sponsored by Marlboro cigarettes. I guess they had saved enough of their empty cigarettes packs to qualify for the sweepstakes. The previous day they had shot a big bull elk on the Indian reservation.

I believe they were from Minnesota. Both were avid trappers. The previous year, he had been named state trapper of the year and his wife won the same honor for the women.

The man did a lot of custom skinning. His home was a local drop-off point for beaver to be skinned. He said it wasn't unusual to come home from work and find a pile of 30 beavers waiting by his garage. He'd been doing it all his life, said it only took a few minutes to skin the animal, scrape the flesh off and put the pelt on a stretcher.

About 10:30 a.m. those nice folks dropped me off several yards from the boat dock. The campground had been flooded so they couldn't get close. I gave them five dollars, but thought afterwards that it was a piddly amount considering the long drive. They said they were happy to help and seemed sincere about it. I waved as they drove off.

About 30 miles away was Chamberlain. That was my goal for the day. The only problem was that my water containers were about empty. In my haste to get around the dam I forgot to fill them. As I approached the highway 47 bridge I gave some fishermen my letters to mail and asked where I could get water. They said there was a casino just up the road.

It was the White Buffalo Casino. They weren't open for the day, but Indian workers were entering through the rear door. I asked about getting my water jugs filled and was told that perhaps the lady at the snack bar could help me out.

I noticed the security camera, but didn't think much about it as I entered. There was a lady busy behind the bar. I told her I knew they were closed, but I was canoeing down the river, in need of drinking water, and didn't have time to wait until they opened. She willingly took my containers. Immediately there were two tough-looking Indian guards on each side of me. They had spotted me on the security camera.

"What you think you're doing in here?"

"I'm just getting my water containers filled."

"We're closed. You're not allowed in here. We'll escort you to the door."

One pointed toward the door I had entered through.

"Can I get my water first?"

The lady said, "Just settle down boys. I'm getting his water."

They finally waited long enough for me to get the water, then followed me to the door.

Good naturedly I said, "Hey guys, I know you got a lot of money in here, but I'm not after that. I'm canoeing down the Missouri to St. Louis and just needed some water."

They had no comment or no smile. Just smartly closed the door behind me.

Halfway to Chamberlain it started to rain. A bass boat went past on the other side of the river. I waved but guess he didn't see me. Later we would meet.

I figured Chamberlain must be close now. There was a father and little boy fishing off the shore. I asked them how far Chamberlain was. Just around the bend, was the reply.

There was a small cove with cement stairs disappearing from the embankment into the water. When I was closer I could see that the stairs led to a cement dock that was underwater.

Above was an RV (recreational vehicle) park. When the big floods hit in 1996 the high water pretty much destroyed the park. It looked like the water level at flood stage was at least 20 feet higher than now. The asphalt roads were all broken apart, trees were down; even the phone booth was tipped over.

It was still raining, but I found a grassy spot and set up the tent. I walked into town. It was Sunday with not much going on, so I thought I'd make a few calls home.

Monday morning it was still raining. It looked like an all-day thing. I cooked up breakfast, put on my rain jacket and walked into town with hopes of finding the library and catching up on all the news since I'd been gone. I didn't find the library but I did pick up a Chamberlain travel brochure that told of a small Indian museum. The museum was a mile away according to the map on the brochure.

Even though it was a small museum it was really interesting. The Akto Lakota Museum had very realistic scenery set up with life-sized Indian figures in different costumes beside stuffed horses and full sized tepees. I shook the rain off my jacket, hung it up and strolled around. There was also a nice collection of artifacts.

There was a lady, probably in her 50's, sitting at the curator's desk. I was the only tourist in the museum today, so I thought I'd go around and say hello. I told her where I was from and about my trip. Also I complimented her on how much I enjoyed the museum. She was very pleasant. "Look around some more and enjoy yourself. Just stay around for a few more minutes."

She picked up the phone and was telling the local newspaper a little bit about my trip. She mentioned that I was still here if they wanted to interview me.

A flash of embarrassment caught my senses. "You didn't have to call the newspaper."

"Oh you go over there and sit down. The reporter will be here in a few minutes," she said.

I just finished watching a video on Indians when the reporter came in. "Are you the guy canoeing the river?" she asked. "I'm Janice Mosel from the Register." Being interviewed by a newspaper reporter was a new experience for me, but her manner immediately made me feel comfortable. She had lots of good questions to carry the conversation. If the article she wrote was as thorough as the interview, it would take up a whole page of the newspaper.

When she was finished, she said that she would like a picture of me by the canoe. I noticed that she had nice clothes on, with open-toe shoes.

"Well it's kinda rainy out there," I said.

"That's all right. I grew up on a farm."

We drove out to the RV park. The entrance was all gated off since the flood damage, so we had to walk in. That meant going through some areas of tall wet grass.

"You sure you want to walk through here?"

She again reminded me of her farm background.

After a picture on the steps by the canoe she asked if I wanted to be dropped off somewhere.

"Sure, if the library isn't out of the way."

I hung out at the library for a couple hours reading newspapers. A man came in with a rain suit on. His hair was all wet. He took off the raincoat, hung it up and came right over to my table.

"You the guy canoeing the river?" he said.

"Yes."

"I'm Gary Carlson. I've been right behind you in a bass boat."

"No kidding! I'd really like to talk to you."

We sat and talked for an hour. You can tell people about things that happen to you on the river, but it is much more meaningful to share those experiences with someone who has that common core of experience. There were a lot of things we didn't talk about. All the helpful people along the way, the sunrises, sunsets, rough water and wildlife. Those were things we didn't need to talk about because they were taken for granted as part of the other man's trip.

We talked about each other's equipment. Gary was traveling the Missouri in a 14-foot bass boat powered by a 24 hp motor. He and his grandfather had bought the boat together many years ago. On a good day he could cover 100 to 150 miles. Just about double the mileage I could. He also had traveled the full length of the Mississippi three years earlier. That impressed me.

Gary told me that his boat was set up so that he could sleep on it. In the bottom he carried four or five fuel tanks covered with plywood to put his bedroll on. He had a tarp or awning arrangement to provide protection from the rain. To go around the dams, he had special wheels that could be attached to the boat with pins. On the bow there was a handle to tie to the back of a vehicle for the tow.

From St. Paul, Minnesota, Gary's business was renovating old buildings, then renting them out. He was 42 years old and before this business he had earned a law degree, practicing for two years in Denver. He said that the law profession was not for him. Originally he had been a carpenter, and that at least gave him some self-satisfaction in life.

We left the library, continuing our discussion over lunch at McDonalds. Gary was not married and said he didn't intend to get married, though he had been dating the same girl for seven years. I really admired this guy. To be in your 40's and still be out doing adventurous things was neat.

It was raining out yet, but Gary planned to continue on down to Sioux City anyway. We shook hands, exchanged addresses and said good-bye. Two complete strangers had met and would probably never see each other again. Yet in only an hour we had established a friendship, an appreciation of what we were individually accomplishing. Maybe there was even a better understanding of why we were each doing it.

We walked back to the river. He started out towards Sioux City while I sat in the tent and wrote some letters. Later I walked back into town for the 9 p.m. movie. It was a scary outer space movie, but still a real treat. There had been no TV or movies for me for a month.

Around 11 p.m. when the movie was over, I walked the 2-1/2 miles back to the tent. It was really dark out as I made my way through the muddy, washed-out park. Even the streetlights down there had been washed out by the big flood.

The next time I talked to Dad he said the Chamberlain newspaper mailed him a copy of the story they did on me and Gary Carlson. It was almost a full-page story with pictures. The headlines were: MODERN DAY FRONTIERSMEN TRAVELING THE MISSOURI.

I was just finishing my breakfast when an old man came up to say hello. We visited for awhile as I packed things up. Before he left he said, "Make sure you stop and take a look at the sulphur vents. They're not too far down river."

The morning was misty when I crossed under the I-90 expressway bridge just south of Chamberlain. I could see the Indian tepee on the hill. Although it had only been a month since I stood up there and saw the Missouri for the first time, it seemed like ages ago. Now I was at least halfway to St. Louis. There were only two more dams on the river to portage around, so I should be able to make good time and be in St. Louis by the end of October. That took some pressure off.

On the east side of the Missouri there were high cliffs. To the west it was rolling prairie. The White River soon joins the Missouri and mixes to change the river color from brown to white. The White River is aptly named, for it picks up white clay particles in its journey across South Dakota and the water is pure white in color.

There was a large boat ahead, so I stayed to the left. The folks inside seemed intent on watching me. The man started the boat's motor and headed in my direction. There were a couple of teenage boys with the man and a young girl. As they pulled alongside I thought about reaching up to grab hold of their boat, but hesitated. It was so dirty looking and reeked of a rotten fish smell.

The fisherman that gave me directions to Chamberlain two days ago was this man's buddy. They had talked about the lone canoeist, so when they saw my canoe he wanted to meet me. He was a commercial fisherman on the Missouri. I told him about my trip and he told me about his fishing operation.

In Michigan, catfish, bullheads and carp, all bottom fish, are not held in high regard by fishermen. Not so here. Those fish are plentiful in the Missouri and when smoked there is a real good market for them. The man told me that in two good days they could bring in almost $8000 worth of fish.

Kettle nets, the size of a cement mixer drum, are baited with rotten cheese and weighted on the bottom of the river. The fish get in the net and can't get out. A string from the net leads to a pop bottle floating on the surface to mark its location.

I'm sure you get used to the smell after awhile, but the sight of dirty catfish and bullheads in those washtubs combined with the residual odors associated with the operation were enough to make me swear off eating fish for awhile.

From two miles away I could see the sulfur vents. They looked like smoky campfires. When I arrived there, it was difficult getting the canoe to shore. Looking down in the water you would swear that there were nice round stones to step on, but in reality they were just balls of soft squishy clay. My feet really sank in.

I thought about climbing up to inspect the basketball-size hole with the white sulphur steam coming out, but it looked too high to climb. Yellow crystal-like pieces of rock had formed all around the hole.

I got out my cookstove, made some soup and ate a sandwich. I started tossing some rocks toward the hole and eventually one of them knocked off some of the crystal. A clod came rolling down the hill towards me. Great! A nice souvenir and I didn't have to climb the hill to get it. The crystal clump hit the wet sand just before I reached down to pick it up. There was a hissing sound like water on a hot frying pan. It's a good thing I didn't just grab that rock or I would have had some burned fingers. I wet the end of one finger and touched it. Ouch!

I spent quite a bit of time at the steam holes that day, but still I covered around 30 miles before I pulled into a little lagoon to camp. There was a road bridge there, a boat ramp, port-a-john and a single light to see by. The only thing noteworthy was that this campsite, and my routine there, would be so typical of most all my overnights for the next month. First I'd put some water on to boil, and in the meantime I'd inflate my mattress, lay out my bedroll and unpack what food I needed. It was usually either romaine noodles, mashed potatoes, rice, stove top stuffing or some other type of noodles along with whatever meat I had. After dinner I'd clean up and read some more of Lewis and Clark's story, **UNDAUNTED COURAGE**, then go to sleep.

In the mornings my bedroll would usually be covered with dew. While the water for hot chocolate boiled, I'd hang up the sleeping bag to dry and start making french toast. I ate french toast morning after morning and still I never tired of it. With real or dried eggs, whichever I happened to have, I'd mix water with the dry milk, add some cinnamon, milk and dip my bread in. The iron skillet I brought along worked great. In 10 minutes I had 5 or 6 slices ready to eat.

I was off by 9 a.m. and planned to make Ft. Randall Dam before dark. There were no lengthy stops that day. My body was now well accustomed to paddling continuously. I could paddle for 3 or 4 hours without stopping and my muscles wouldn't even notice. Once I calculated that on a good day I would take 12,000 strokes with the paddle.

Late in the day on the north shore I saw a parked RV. There were two guys sitting there in armchairs drinking beer with the radio playing loud. I paddled over to see how much farther the dam was. When they saw me approaching, one got right up and came down to greet me. He was middle-aged, slightly balding with blond hair and was quite cheerful. The other guy eventually came down too, bringing an extra beer. He was middle-aged too, slightly balding with blond hair and cheerful too. These guys were just too cheerful. In fact, I think they were gay. No other tourists in sight, or fishing poles. Just time together in the middle of the week in the RV.

Well I hung around for 20 minutes, drank the beer they brought me and we watched a nice sunset. They said it was another 10 miles to the dam, so I thanked them for the beer and left.

It was pitch black and I could see a strobe light on the north shore. There was a big lagoon there and the light marked the end of a rock breaker wall put in place to protect the boats in the lagoon. I couldn't detect the wall until I was close and could hear the water slapping the rocks.

After making my way along to the end of the breaker wall, I entered the lagoon to find a fancy boat dock area with lots of expensive looking cabin cruisers and sailboats. Except for a couple of streetlights it was dark. There were several no trespassing keep out signs. It looked like some kind of yacht club.

Quietly I paddled up between a couple of boats and tied the canoe off. I didn't unload, just ate a quick sandwich and a piece of sausage. There was a trailer up there with a light on. Thought I'd go up and say hello, maybe see how welcome I would be. I knocked on the door. No answer. The door was unlocked so I opened it, peeked in and hollered, "Hello!" Still no answer, but then I noticed the note on the door. GONE TO THE BAR WILL BE BACK.

I really needed a hot shower and to do some laundry. There was another building with showers and a washing machine. With the lights off I climbed into the hot shower. Wow, did that feel good. What a pleasure it would be to be clean again. After the shower I shaved, brushed my teeth and put my dirties in the machine. I kept a watch outside. The yacht club members might not appreciate me freeloading their utilities.

Between two dry-docked sailboats, I put up a makeshift clothesline to dry my clothes. I laid out the bedroll down by the boat dock. The wind picked up and on the hill I could see my clothes moving around with the wind. During the night I could hear cars coming down the gravel road and turning around at the dock. My bedroll was in the shadows on the end of the dock so they couldn't see me.

This was not a good place to sleep. I tucked the canoe under the dock, picked up my mattress with the sleeping bag, and relocated behind the trailer wheels of a dry-docked sailboat. The wind had really picked up and the trailer wheels would give me some protection. Some of my laundry had already blown off on the grass. Even though it was only half dry I packed it away. Finally I went to sleep, waking up only once when the trailer guy came home from the bar.

Before daylight I left the yacht club. According to the map I had five miles before the Ft. Randall Dam. Just before the dam I found another lagoon. There was a fisherman there trying to get his boat motor started. A four-foot-thick fog bank covered the water. I switched into my stealth paddling mode, heading directly at the fisherman. Quietly I glided up behind him. "Good morning!" He jumped a little then said, "You snuck up behind me." He told me where the boat ramp was. There was kind of a weird shaped peninsula where I tied the canoe. To get to it someone would have to hop over a bunch of logs, walk through mud and crawl out on a branch. I was starving so I thought I'd walk into Pickstown for breakfast. That was a big mistake. The town was farther away than I thought. About five miles worth.

It was harvest time and along the highway corn had jostled out of the farmers' gravity box wagons on the way to town. I picked up a few kernels. Chewed up they tasted just like corn bread. When cars weren't going by I would reach down and pick up more to eat. By the time I reached the restaurant, I had devoured a couple handfuls of corn. Certainly I wasn't starving anymore, but I was still hungry. The restaurant was empty. I ordered three pancakes and the waitress questioned whether I wanted that many, "They're pretty big." I told her I was hungry.

When the pancakes arrived each was as big or bigger than the plate. Still, I ate them all.

Next to the restaurant was a full service gas station. There was an elderly gentleman busy washing the windshield for a customer. I asked him if he knew of someone who would help me portage around the dam. He said he'd be with me in a minute.

Inside the station was an old hound dog. From my breakfast I had saved a strip of bacon for a later treat. It was wrapped in a napkin in my pocket. Old hound dog came up wagging his tail. He liked the smell of my pocket. It certainly must have brightened up his morning when I gave in to his hunger with my strip of bacon. Then I added to his pleasure with a good back scratch all the way down to the top of his butt.

The old man came in. "Well it looks like you made a good friend. Are you ready to go?"

"Oh, are you going to take me then?"

"Yep. The mechanic is going to watch things."

He took some stuff out of the back of the truck to make room for my canoe. "Over the years I guess I've helped about two or three others around the dam. The last one was three years ago."

Old hound dog and I rode in back with the canoe. It was almost two miles around the dam to the boat ramp. There were trees on both sides of the ramp and water was pouring out of the dam. I looked forward to a fast-flowing river again.

We unloaded the canoe and he said, "Have a nice day," and left. That's the extent of our conversation. You would have thought he ran a daily shuttle back and forth, not once every three years or longer.

There was a van parked by the boat ramp. A heavy lady got out and went over to use the park toilet. The man was sharpening a knife at the table outside the van. I said hello and found out that he was a butcher by trade. My knife was getting dull; I inquired if he could sharpen it.

"I'd be happy to."

From Ft. Randall Dam the river becomes the border between South Dakota and Nebraska. My destination was Niobrara, where I planned to camp and find a restaurant for supper.

The Niobrara River travels across a good share of Nebraska and enters the Missouri around the town of Niobrara. I was not impressed with the river at that point. It was laden with clods of algae and smelled like dead fish. This area was also the start of Lewis and Clark Lake which was the backwater from the next and last Missouri dam, Gavins Point Dam. There was a field of cattails between me and the shoreline. Using the sound of boats on the river and automobile noise from the town to get my bearings, I tried several different channels through the seven-foot-high cattails to reach the shoreline. Each time I ran into a dead end. Disgusted, I finally tried to pole my way right across the cattails, but that was just a lot of extra work which only got me back out to the main channel again.

There was a boat out there, trying like I was to find the boat ramp. It was too shallow for them to try the channels I had been exploring. Finally I found my way to land. It was about six inches higher than the water. When I came up to the shoreline I saw there was an old beat up pickup truck. Close to the truck there was a john boat with five fishing lines in the water. The fisherman had been napping, but was now staring at me as I approached. "You went through my fishing lines," he said in a grumpy voice.

"Sorry, I tried to avoid them. Can you tell me where the boat ramp is?"

"Down there, keep goin'."

The boat ramp was a half slab of concrete, nothing elaborate. I buttoned up the canoe and covered it with my army blanket. The place was infested with mosquitos. I unbuttoned the canoe again and sprayed myself good with OFF.

Niobrara was two miles away, located on a small hill. The mosquitos were not as bad on the road, but when I took a shortcut across a baseball field they were all over me. I was carrying the two water jugs, so swatting the attackers was more of a challenge.

At a gas station I got out my calling card and talked to the answering machines and Renae. She said that she and Aunt Shelby had a very nice trip together out west.

The lady at the gas station told me where the town's most popular restaurant was. It closed at 9 p.m. and it was already around 8:30. When I walked in, the place still had several customers. They all stared at me. I was the stranger and people like to stare at strangers. With my river hat and sunglasses around my neck I just looked out of place. There were some old men talking and drinking coffee at one table and some farmers with their wives and kids at the other tables. Their staring continued as I ate my dinner, but by now I was used to it. I finished off my meal with my favorite strawberry malt.

After the waitress brought the malt she said, "You're not from around here, are you?"

"Nope. I'm canoeing the Missouri to St. Louis. Started on the Yellowstone in Billings, Montana." I could see the ears prick up at the neighboring tables. I certainly did not welcome any lengthy discussions tonight. I had a two mile walk back to the canoe.

The waitress disappeared into the kitchen. With the malt polished off, I glanced at the newspaper while I patiently waited for my bill.

A lady about 65 came out of the kitchen and over to my table. She looked like the cook, probably the owner too. There was no hello. She just started right out, "I can't believe you're canoeing the whole Missouri, and eating in my restaurant too. Are you spending the night?"

"Well, I'm not sure yet."

She continued, "Well if you do I want you to come up here and I'll cook you a real good breakfast."

"OK."

As I stood up to pay the bill she gave me a big hug and said, "Good luck and God bless. I'll pray for you."

I thanked her in as sincere a manner as I could. Everyone was taking this in and if I didn't want to get stuck I had to make a fast exit.

Despite the mosquitos, my plan was to cut back across the ball field. Not far behind a car seemed to be following me. It had an antenna and a big spotlight on the side. Must be the local police investigating the stranger. I walked right over to the driver's side and said, "You must be the local police." Two men sat in the front seat in T-shirts and shorts. The driver said, "Well, yes. We're the police, fire department and town paramedics. Where ya headed?"

I told them I was walking back to the river and gave them a condensed version of my trip. They asked a couple questions, then one remarked that the river was quite a walk from here. I acknowledged that and then there was some silence before the light bulb went on. "You want a ride?"

"Boy that would really help out. It's late and the mosquitos are mean tonight."

They really drove slow on the two track back to the river. We saw some muskrats in the headlights and when the cruiser lights hit the canoe it looked like nobody had messed with it. We visited a minute, then they wished me luck and left.

Instantly I dove for the mosquito spray. Either I had to immediately take refuge in my sleeping bag or look for a better place to camp. I chose the latter.

When I passed the guy's camper trailer that had snapped at me about his fishing lines, I could hear him and his wife arguing inside. Maybe he had a reason to be ornery.

I found the channel and could see a boat light out in the river. I could also hear voices. The people had an interior boat light on to get some more beer out of the cooler. It sounded like they were doing more drinking than fishing. I quietly glided up to their boat as they switched the light back off.

I was right beside the boat before one of the ladies saw this white shape coming out of the darkness. "Goodness, George. What's that?"

"Hello!" I said. "Just had dinner in Niobrara. The mosquitos were eating me up and I'm looking for a better campsite."

There were two couples in the boat. One guy was big and feisty with a beard and long dark hair. He invited me aboard to join them for a couple beers. We talked until 1 a.m. Then they said they'd have to leave for home. They warned me about the bridge construction going on. There were a lot of barges and equipment in the river just ahead. I could hear the water rushing around it from where we were.

Going around barges was dangerous in the daytime, let alone at night. There wasn't a lot of current, but enough to suck you under or create some nice eddies at the rear of the barge. The folks told me that just a month before, a single barge with a crane on it had flipped over, pinning the operator on the bottom of the river, drowning him.

These good folks told me to follow them. They would guide me past the equipment. With a spotlight we slowly made our way through. It was cold out now and we all had our jackets on.

When they pulled the boat out, there was just a partial dock. Not enough to sleep on, but there didn't seem to be many mosquitoes so I could just put my bedroll on the ground. The couples wished me luck and said good night.

I was officially on the Lewis and Clark Lake with 30 miles to go to the Gavins Point Dam. The lake was miserably shallow with a strong quartering tail wind. Right out in the middle of the lake I continually got stuck on sand bars. There were high cliffs on the south side, so to get away from the wind, I headed across. Believe me, it was a struggle to make the other side.

Around noon I found a park that a bunch of prisoners, all wearing orange uniforms, were cleaning up. The river floods of '96 had taken their toll everyplace and this was just another project to fix things back up.

With all the sand bars, I had been in and out of the canoe several times. The waves had splashed a lot of water in when the cover was open, so now I took everything out to dry. I had lunch, used the restroom and was soon on my way again.

Things were more enjoyable that afternoon. I paddled the south side enjoying the scenery along these high cliffs. Towards the south end of the lake a fisherman told me of a large boat ramp and marina on the other side. The wind was still blowing good, so again I was abused by the waves as I struck out for the marina.

A large breaker wall protected the marina. Inside were some very expensive yachts and sailboats. I would guess that many were worth over a half million dollars. I asked a man onshore about getting some help around the dam. He directed me to a large dry-dock warehouse. Inside I met an Army Corps of Engineers employee. He said that it was no problem for them to get me around the dam. The man asked a younger fellow to take me, and before long I was below the dam and in the fast current to Yankton.

There were some nice big sand bars in the river and I considered setting up my tent on one. The problem was that most of them were lousy with spiders. I decided to continue to Yankton.

Yankton is an attractive city. There is a boardwalk from the river right up to the town square. Some very nice homes are built into the hills around the city.

I tied the canoe to the dock and walked up in the square for some water and supplies. There seemed to be a lot of people around. At Burger King I had dinner, then a strawberry malt at the Dairy Queen. There were several historical markers so I wandered around reading them.

The dock area was too close to town. I didn't figure they'd appreciate me sleeping there, so I paddled on looking for a more appropriate place.

Past the downtown area I saw a 10- or 12-year-old boy fishing from a dock. He was all excited over the small catfish he had just hauled up. I went over and I could see he wasn't quite sure how to get the hook out without getting stung. "That's a nice fish you've got there. Would you like my pliers to get that hook out?"

"Gee, thanks." I handed him the pliers. In short order he had the hook out and tossed the fish back in the water.

"Say, do you know a good place where I could camp tonight?"

"Well, right here wouldn't be a bad spot."

"Good. I'm really tired."

"Where you comin' from?" he asked.

"From Billings, Montana. I'm headed to St. Louis."

"Really?" He was impressed and asked several questions about the trip.

A couple of this guy's buddies came riding down and parked their bikes beside his on the dock. I could see that this conversation was going to continue for sometime, so I tried to talk to all of them while I unpacked. Sometimes I would get tired of telling people about this trip, but these boys were young, impressionable and eager to hear my story, so how could I not take time to answer their questions?

This was not a particularly good area. There was a small pavilion not far away with some teenagers drinking beer and raising hell. I worried about having these young kids here with those party animals so close.

I fired up the stove and made some hot chocolate. The boys thought my stove was cool. I tried to tell them both the good and bad points of my journey.

It was after 10 p.m. when the young boys left. They warned me to be careful because some bum comes down to fish off this dock quite often. I was more worried about the drinking teenagers. They were breaking beer bottles on the rocks now and getting louder and louder. I laid back on the bedroll, but didn't dare go to sleep.

When I woke up it was about 2 a.m., but my world was completely lit up. Three police cruisers sat on shore with their lights all pointed at me. What woke me up was the footsteps of an officer walking down the dock towards my sleeping bag.

"What you doing here?" he asked.

"Well I was sleeping until you got here."

"Why are you here?"

"I'm canoeing down the river from Billings, Montana."

About that time he spotted my canoe and yelled back to the other officers, "He canoed here all the way from Billings, Montana!"

"Where ya headed?"

"I'm on my way to St. Louis."

"He's going all the way to St. Louis!" he again shouted to the others.

"I can't let you sleep out here. Now that I've checked on you, if you roll off the dock and drown it's my fault."

"Gee, I've been sleeping on docks for a month with no problem."

He went on to explain that someone had spotted the canoe, thought it was loose and called in about it. When they arrived they saw this lump on the dock and thought it might be someone who was hurt.

The officer said he'd radio in and see if his supervisor would mind me sleeping there tonight. The dispatcher checked and radioed back, "It's OK, just tell him not to roll off the dock."

I told the officer about the big party at the pavilion and that it would be nice if they'd occasionally check the area through the night. He said he would. The other two police cruisers left but this officer wanted more details about my trip. We talked for about 20 minutes and finally in between yawns I said I'd have to go to sleep because I had a full day of canoeing planned for the next day.

"I understand," he said. He gave me his card. Through the night I woke up a couple times as a cruiser came by and flashed the lights around, checking on things. Before dozing off for good, I thought, Yankton is a nice town, nice people. Just another day on the river.

The Bell Takes A Dive

September 27th to September 30th

It was not a great night's sleep, but I still felt pretty good and was busy cooking breakfast when the first two boys arrived. They had backpacks on, so obviously some kind of camping trip was in the works. More boys started arriving, all with backpacks. They seemed to be around 10 to 15 years old. A lady came over and inquired where I was canoeing to. I gave her some details and asked where the boys were going today. She said that their scout troop was headed off on a three-day canoe trip to Sioux City. They would be leaving shortly.

Pretty soon vans and trucks came, bringing more boys and a dozen older looking aluminum canoes. There was a lot of hustle and bustle as canoes and equipment were being unloaded. Between overly helpful parents and a bunch of excited scouts, there appeared to be a severe lack of organization.

One man seemed to be the scout leader and in charge, though his efforts were having little effect on order. I had a good laugh over his outfit. His hat looked like the old triangular pirate hats we used to make from paper. His was made out of cotton and it looked pretty raggedy. He wore green cutoff shorts. Not only did he look a little comical, his mannerisms were like those of Gomer Pyle.

A couple of the scouts came over and asked questions about my trip. After leaving, I could see them over whispering to their buddies. Pretty soon a few more came over.

When I took my dishes up to wash them off at the water faucet, I saw the lady I had originally visited with. I guess she was the scout leader's wife. As several of the boys were curious about my trip, I told her that if she would get them all together before I left, I would be willing to answer any questions they might have. "Great," she said.

"Gather the boys around in a circle. I'll finish packing up my canoe, then come over and talk with them."

While I was packing up, a local newspaper reporter arrived on the scene and started asking me questions. He's there to report on the scouts' trip, but decides he wants to do a story on me too. His photographer, a woman, was busy snapping my picture. Finally I asked the reporter to come over for my visit with the scouts, as he could probably get enough information for his story there.

The reporter introduced me to the group. It was a good-sized gathering, probably 25 scouts plus parents and the reporters.

"Good morning. I'm Scott Galloway, canoeing from Billings, Montana, 2400 miles to St. Louis, Missouri and having the time of my life. Would you like to ask any questions about my trip?" I think about every hand went up.

It seemed like I answered 150 questions. I tried to give an in-depth response to each question. They asked about my equipment, the food I took along, was I scared alone on the river, everything. I spent at least an hour answering questions and received a nice round of applause at the end.

The boys paired off in the canoes. Several asked if I would canoe part way with them. I said I would catch up with them in a few minutes. The reporter had some additional questions and his assistant snapped a few more pictures. There were several parents still around when I left. They all waved a nice good-bye to me.

About 20 minutes later I caught up with the scouts. The leader with the triangular pirate's hat was bringing up the rear. I could tell he was annoyed by my presence. Earlier he acted miffed because I was talking to his boys and now I was getting the cold shoulder.

Maybe he thought I delayed their departure too much, or perhaps he just thought I threatened his status with the boys. Anyway, I just continued paddling alongside of him, trying to carry on a conversation. The scouts allowed their canoes to drift back with us and that seemed to irritate him a little more. Finally everyone stopped at a sand bar for a break and I said good-bye.

Speaking to the scouts was a good experience for me. They were interested in what I had to say and asked intelligent questions. It made me feel a little like a celebrity and at the same time it added some meaning to my trip.

Sioux City, Iowa was my goal for the day. It was about 70 miles away, but there was a decent current and I planned to set a good pace paddling. I had heard about all the casino boats there. It might be fun to gamble a little.

I was about 10 miles from Sioux City and could see a large cloud mass in that direction. The radio station was saying that Sioux City had taken a pounding and I was a little worried that I might have to encounter the storm before I arrived there. The sun was just starting to set in the west.

There was development along the river now and man-made barriers protecting the shoreline from erosion. The opportunity to pull out of the river on short notice would be very limited because of those rock barriers. I was worried about being caught out on the river in a storm. The wind was already starting to pick up.

Three guys in a motorboat pulled alongside and asked where I was headed. They were worried about the storm too and offered to tow my canoe or bring it right up on board their boat. Their boat was too high and the canoe too heavy, so one of the men said, "Let's put a line on and pull it." I buttoned down the cover and tied a line to the front, then climbed on their boat.

The man driving was tall, missing some front teeth and a bit grumpy. The curly-haired guy with a medium build was riding in back with me along with a 14-year-old boy.

We attached the tow rope to a tie-down fitting on the boat, then I held the rope to help absorb any jerks on the line. We started out, but the canoe was not riding the wake. The rope was too short. An additional line was added to the existing one, so now we had around 100 feet of line. At 25 mph the canoe was now riding the wake nicely.

The tall guy driving yelled back, "Everything OK?" The curly-haired guy responded, "It's goin' good."

I'm not sure whether the driver was overly concerned with the storm or just wanted to go faster. He shoved the throttle way forward and we were going close to 40 mph. The canoe now went crazy, tearing from side to side. I couldn't control it.

I yelled, "Stop!"

The driver chopped the throttle, which immediately slowed the boat, but not the canoe. There was no wake now. The canoe dug in and knifed into the river. It went out of sight all the way to the river bottom. It disappeared for 10 seconds then slowly the trapped air in the flotation cavities forced it to the surface. The snaps on the cover had popped open and it was full of water. My gun hung over the side, still attached to a safety lanyard. It had been a nice day so I hadn't tied up my food bag. Everything was soaked. Only one bag of clothes and my sleeping bag were dry.

The canoe had a big chip out of one side and both sides were cracked. As I was surveying the damage the driver said, "That was there before. We didn't do that."

"No it wasn't," I responded.

Now they just wanted to leave me and be on their way. The tall guy ran the spotlight along shore, but you could see nothing but jagged rocks. There was a pretty good-sized sand bar ahead about 100 feet from shore. I told them to just let me out on the sand bar. The wind was from behind and the three foot waves pushed the boat up on the sand bar.

I removed enough of my stuff from the canoe so that it could be tipped over and drained. The damaged area would allow some water to come in, but I thought I could make it to Sioux City. Quickly I packed the canoe and snapped the cover on. Meanwhile, the other guys were trying to get the motorboat unbeached from the sand bar. They were still there when I pushed off.

Soon I met another boat coming up river. Their spotlight caught me and they came over close. It was a river rescue boat. Someone onshore had reported that there was a boat in distress. I told them that I had some damage and was taking on a little water, but could make it to Sioux City. The other boat was not damaged, just stuck on a sand bar.

The river coast guard decided they'd follow me into Sioux City. I found a boat ramp close to a big motel, and that's where I spent the night. There was a place to wash and dry my clothes, but other than that, I just took out of the canoe what I needed for the night. It was Saturday night and I didn't look forward to the next day. The canoe would have to be repaired before I continued and how much luck I would have finding repair materials on Sunday was the big question. There was a bar close by, so I had one beer to unwind then crawled into my dry sleeping bag and passed out. What a day.

The next morning I emptied out the canoe and laid my stuff out in the sun to dry. It was a mess. Most of the food was ruined, but from what I could tell, the only thing that was missing was my tent poles. That was no big deal because I had been sleeping on docks a good share of the time anyway. Only if it rained a lot would that be a problem. My film was probably ruined. That had been underwater along with all my letter writing material. I hated to write letters anyway, so good riddance to that stuff.

I would need some bondo to fix the break in the canoe. That should work OK over the Kevlar. When I thought they might be open, I started walking to find an auto parts store. It seemed like I walked at least six miles, but eventually I found one open.

Back at the boat ramp, I had just started to get things ready to repair the canoe when this guy pulls up in a pickup truck with his family. He surveys the situation and asks if I could use some help repairing the canoe. He works in an auto body repair shop. What a godsend this guy was. When we finished you could hardly see where the canoe had been damaged. The paint even matched. And if that wasn't enough, he took me to the grocery store to replace my damaged food supply. His wife and kids watched my stuff while we were gone.

I can't say enough about how much this guy did in my time of need. Not only did he do a superior job repairing my canoe, he saved me time and was instrumental in putting me back on the river as if nothing bad had happened. I tried and tried to make him take pay, but he wouldn't consider it. This family had unselfishly taken a chunk out of their Sunday to help a stranger. I felt humbled by their kindness. They were all lined up along the riverbank waving when I pushed out into the river.

My journey would be different now in many respects. On either the left or right side of the river, there would be a sign each mile telling the miles remaining to St. Louis. From Sioux City, I believe the first sign said 749 miles to go. In some respects this was good, for I could easily gauge my speed and know that I was already several days ahead of schedule. On the other hand, watching the miles click off one by one was not what I'd call exciting.

The river was still the boundary line between states. Before Sioux City it had separated Nebraska and South Dakota. Now it was the border for Nebraska and Iowa.

I had always envisioned Nebraska as being low and flat. Along the river that was not the case. On the Nebraska side there was a 50 to 100 foot embankment, while the Iowa side was flat.

Because of the numerous dams, there was no barge traffic above Sioux City on the Missouri. Below the Missouri there would be many barges hauling everything, from grain, coal, mineral ore and oil. A common sight along the river now would be huge power plants, refineries and grain elevators. Not exactly Lewis and Clark scenery, but a result of their exploration and the continual commercial development of the west. The Missouri was the gateway then, and obviously still maintains that status now, even if in a lesser form.

Even though I started late, I got 40 miles under my belt and spent the night at a boat ramp near the road bridge in Decatur, Nebraska. The stretch of river I covered that day was pretty remote. There were no towns near the river, no rivers or creeks that entered the Missouri, just the high ground of Nebraska on the west and the flat land of Iowa to the east.

At my camp area I did see the first snake of the trip. It was a four-foot-long garter snake. Before I even started this trip I had been paranoid about encountering poisonous snakes. Renae had even purchased me a snakebite kit. People I talked to nourished my fears, for they said September was the worst month for snake bites. That's the month the snakes shed their skin. It somehow limits their sight and they will strike at any disturbance. At first when I went hunting through brush, I was constantly watching and poking ahead with a stick. For over a month I had seen no snakes, nor had anyone else I talked to. That fear was pretty much behind me now.

It was Monday, September 29th, my 26th birthday. I would try to reach Omaha and call home so everyone could wish me happy birthday. The folks had sent cards along for me to open, but it was still kind of a long, lonely day just the same. Once again there were no towns along the river.

I thought that I had seen a lot of pelicans on the Yellowstone, but the numbers were nothing compared to what I was seeing now. They must be migrating, for I would routinely see a couple hundred perched on a sand bar. They would even hang out near barges and docks.

Just south of Blair, Nebraska, there was an interesting wildlife refuge depicted on the Iowa side. You could leave the river and paddle around a loop through the refuge, but if I was to make Omaha to call home I wouldn't have time to stop. I continued on.

Even though I was making good time it became obvious I wouldn't make Omaha before dark. I still had this burning desire to call home. After all, it was still my birthday and as much as I needed to hear from home I wanted them to know that I was safe. I found a small stream inlet and paddled up that until I came upon a private residence. It was almost dark when I knocked on the door. I wasn't sure how warm the reception would be.

An elderly gentleman came to the door. His wife stood in the background. I introduced myself, told the man what I was doing and that it was my birthday. I asked if I could use his phone to call home. Even though I looked and probably smelled like a river rat, without hesitation he allowed me right into his home.

It was the only birthday present I needed. Just hearing the voices of home was enough. I visited with this couple for a few minutes and thanked them before I left. Back near the river I found an old dock to tie the canoe to and laid out my bedroll on it. It was a pleasant evening and the river seemed peaceful. I would start early in the morning and have breakfast somewhere in Omaha.

Along the river from now to St. Louis, I would see fishing lines attached to tree limbs and marked with plastic pop bottles. A stretch of fish lines was referred to as a trot line. This morning there was a fisherman in a john boat busy checking his lines to see what he might have caught overnight. I paddled over to say hello and see if he might be able to recommend a good breakfast restaurant close to the river.

The fisherman told me that he was a minor league baseball player in Omaha. This was his day off. I thought that he really looked like a pro baseball player too; tall, mustache, baseball cap, sunglasses. Looked like he worked out regularly too. He said the best place to eat breakfast would be on one of the casino boats. They had all-you-could-eat buffets at reasonable prices.

I could see the Omaha skyline from a long ways off. I still had ten miles to go and I was hungry. There was something else in front of me coming up river. I didn't have my glasses on, but I could tell it was a barge. It was the first barge traffic I was to encounter. I read about how dangerous barges were in the book **MISSISSIPPI SOLO**. Other people I talked to confirmed the hazards associated with them. The up river barges were the most dangerous because the tugboats had to work harder to push their heavy loads upstream. The advice from everyone was to just get out of the river, don't mess with them. The tugboats have huge diesel engines with twin four-foot brass and steel propellers that draw a large volume of water towards them. So much in fact, that little inlets to the river will lose all their water as the tug passes, then fill back up again. One guy told me he headed up a tributary to avoid a barge and as it passed the water level went down two feet and his boat was left on bare rocks.

When I put my glasses on it looked like the whole shoreline was moving with the barge formation. It was still three-quarters of a mile away, but I could see diesel smoke pouring out of the tugboat that was pushing the barges. To be on the safe side I would get out now.

I pulled the canoe up on shore. It was a low swampy area and I was right in the middle of a growth of pea pod-shaped sticktights. They were imbedded every place on my clothes.

Actually I pulled out way too early. These barges move about as slow as a person on a leisurely walk. I had to wait 20 minutes before they passed. This was the biggest barge formation I would encounter on the Missouri. There were eight of them cabled together; two abreast, four deep. Six to eight foot waves rose behind the hard working tug that was pushing. It was strange for there was very little noise ahead of the formation, but plenty for a half-hour after it passed. I could see that anything near would be sucked into those props and spit out the rear. Certainly the riverbank was the only safe place to be.

Near downtown I could see two large casino boats. Heading over towards them I saw a parking lot. There was a shade tree near the river with an older man sitting under it and that looked like a good place to go ashore.

Even though it was around 9:30 a.m. the casino parking lot looked full. The old guy under the shade tree was watching me. I hollered, "Good morning!" and waved. He waved back, got up using his cane and came over to help find a good spot for me to pull out. It was rather shallow, but I found a small drainage ditch from the parking lot and entered that.

Could he tell me a good place to eat breakfast, I asked. "Sure," he said, "I'll take you."

We took our time walking to the nearby casino boat. The man was retired and did volunteer work in some kind of mentor program. Regularly he would come down and kill some time by putting a few bucks in the slot machines.

The breakfast line was a 20-minute wait. We visited about my trip while we stood in line. He said that he used to be a reporter and that I should tell my story to the newspaper. I said that I was glad he thought it was interesting, but I didn't care about looking up a newspaper. When we reached the cashier he pulled out his wallet and insisted on buying me breakfast, using his senior citizen discount. After paying he said he enjoyed talking to me and wished me luck.

"Aren't you going to eat breakfast with me?"

"No, I've already had breakfast. I just wanted to get the discount for you."

He shook my hand and left. People never fail to amaze me with their generosity. Here was just one more example of that kindness.

Wow, what a breakfast this was going to be. As the waitress led me to a table, I gazed in wonder at all the food; Belgian waffles, sausage, eggs, all kinds of fresh fruit.

Here I was in my river clothes again, carhart shorts and a T-shirt. Not dressed for this crowd. People were staring but I didn't give a rip. I just hung my river hat on the back of the chair and headed for the food.

I had just polished off my second big plateful from the buffet and was enjoying a good cup of coffee when the waitress approached. In a voice loud enough for all the adjoining tables to hear she said, "You're supposed to return this call to a man at the TV station." She laid a card with the guy's name and number on the table.

The more I thought about it, I decided that I didn't feel comfortable calling some TV reporter down to do a story on me. After finishing my coffee I fished out some money for a tip and left. Part way out the door I remembered I'd left the business card on the table. Even though I had reservations, to be polite I should at least call the reporter. The old man that bought me breakfast must have told them about my trip. I went back, but my table was cleared off and the card was gone.

As I came down the casino boat ramp, I looked across the parking lot to where I tied the canoe by the tree. There were two TV news vans in place and technicians were busy setting up camera equipment. I hadn't even phoned the reporter, but here they were already. Maybe they were there for some other reason. Guess I'd soon find out.

As I walked up one of the TV men spotted me and associated me with the canoe. He came over, pinned a mike on my shirt, and started asking me questions. How far had I come? I answered about 1500 miles. All the questions were standard, with the same answers I had given so many times to so many people before.

Then there was this really cute female reporter. She moved in asking questions while the man stood on the sidelines. I don't know whether I just wasn't used to the TV interview setting or it was her manner, but she would ask me a question then look off into space. Of course the TV camera was on me when I answered her question, but she acted like she wasn't interested in my answer; like she wasn't part of the conversation. It seemed like I was talking to myself and for some reason it pissed me off. This trip might not be a big deal to her, but for me it was. I had started 2,000 miles from home on rivers

I knew little about that were dangerous. I had been thoroughly scared on more occasions than I cared to remember and the day before my canoe dove to the bottom of the Missouri River. Of course I remained cool and didn't say anything disrespectful, but some mean thoughts did present themselves, especially when she rolled her eyes around and looked at the ground during one of my answers.

The cameraman wanted some shots as I pushed off into the river. Then they shouted out, "Would you mind paddling back upstream so we can get you coming by?"

I paddled back up a hundred yards then waved as I went by and the cameras rolled. I didn't know whether any of this would be on the news or not; I really didn't care, for I was weary of this experience.

The river passes near the Omaha Airport and the jet's flight path seemed real low and close to me.

This area was like an industrial park, with a lot of barge traffic. Barges passing downstream didn't present a problem. I would just stay near shore and head directly into the wake as it passed.

Passing by Omaha, I listened to an AM radio station that seemed to be the audio from the TV station that interviewed me. I wondered if they would say anything about my trip on the 5 p.m. news.

Fifteen miles south of Omaha there is a bridge that crosses the river near Bellevue. The river current was quite fast and it was a bit difficult getting up to the shore. There was a creek inlet there. I paddled up that for a ways to a campground and brought the canoe up on a sand bar. I really needed a shower badly. Probably just all the sweat from the TV interview. I smiled to myself. Maybe that's why the TV lady kept turning her head away. Couldn't stand the smell of the river rat.

I took advantage of the campground shower room, then put on some clean clothes and floated back down the creek to the river.

A cement platform connected the pylons under the bridge. It was about eight feet high and six feet wide. That would make a neat place to spend the night if I could figure a way to get up there. I threw up what gear I'd needed, then found a log to prop against the platform.

I spent the afternoon writing in my journal and then tuned in to hear the 5 p.m. news. The broadcast was definitely the TV station audio, but there was nothing about me until the last minute, then the man said, "How about a 1500 mile canoe trip for a vacation? Here's Scott Galloway from Michigan canoeing the Missouri to St. Louis. There will be more on our 10 p.m. news."

I was slightly disgusted, because he said it was a 1500 mile trip and it was really 2400 miles. Well, I'd certainly try to tune in at 10 p.m. and see how much more they had on.

It was 1-1/2 miles into Bellevue. I picked up a few groceries and called Renae. Told her I was a TV star. I had dinner, with dessert at the Dairy Queen. A strawberry malt, of course.

To protect the canoe from water level changes created by the barge traffic, I took it up the inlet and pulled it onshore. It was dark now, so I crawled up the log to my sleeping perch on the platform and settled into my bedroll for the night. At 10 p.m. I tuned in the news.

It was almost 10:30 before they brought my interview on. I checked my watch. It lasted 3-1/2 minutes. They put on what they thought were the interesting parts; the canoe underwater and damage story; going to the bar for a beer afterwards and a few of the complimentary remarks I had made about the nice people of Omaha. I especially thanked the retired reporter that bought me breakfast. All in all I was satisfied with the coverage.

A series of red and green lights marked the path for the barge traffic under the bridge. I slept soundly under the red lights that night, waking up only once about 3 a.m. when a barge went by. I knew the canoe was up high enough to be safe, so in a worry free state of mind I slipped back to sleep.

A Tourist

October 1st to October 7th

Not far south of Omaha the Platte River joins the Missouri. The Platte crosses a good share of Nebraska and is quite wide, but very shallow. They say you can walk across it without getting your hair wet and I think that's a fact.

The Nebraska side of the Missouri continued to have high terrain with more trees than the Iowa side. The river ran at a good speed now and I was again away from civilization. At least I thought I was.

Not too far past the highway bridge east of Plattsmouth, it was necessary for me to make an unplanned stop to the east side of the river. Just returning from the brush, I was pushing the canoe out and from a passing bass boat came, "There's that guy that's canoeing to St. Louis!" I looked up and recognized the man behind the voice.

"Hey! There's the baseball player from Omaha."

The last time I saw this guy was on the north side of Omaha. We met out in the river and he introduced me to his fishing buddy. We visited again for awhile, then I continued my journey and he continued his fishing run. It was the first time since I started this trip that I saw someone for a second time. That doesn't sound like a big deal, but after five weeks on the river, seeing a familiar friendly face puts a nice stamp of happiness on the day.

I camped near Nebraska City. It was one of those times when I couldn't seem to find a good campsite. I kept pushing on and it was getting darker out. Finally I found a small tributary that was only a foot deep and five feet wide. I paddled up that a ways, then unloaded just what I needed for supper. I put my air mattress on the grass.

My last meal had been early in the afternoon. I was starved. I cooked up a package of spaghetti and emptied out a whole jar of sauce. I sat there in the dark just gorging myself. Up on the opposite creek bank I heard a rustling sound. Something was coming through the brush. I found the flashlight and pointed it up in the direction of the noise. There sat five raccoons, all were on their haunches watching me; guess my spaghetti smelled good. With my flashlight still shining in their faces, I tossed a rock up towards them. They still sat there.

I turned the light off then started to brush my teeth. The gurgling sound of the stream seemed to change. I put my toothbrush down and turned the flashlight on again. The five raccoons were coming across the stream. They were intent on having a spaghetti supper. I tossed a few more pebbles in their direction, which finally drove them off for good.

I left very early the next morning. I didn't even eat breakfast. The town of Brownville would be coming up soon and by that time a restaurant should be open. I had a craving for a big country breakfast sitting at a table.

Brownville was a little old town, which according to some sign was established in 1854. There were big grain storage silos down by the river and old historic-looking houses were built on the hill overlooking the river. It wasn't a real prosperous looking place anymore. Almost like a ghost town. Maybe because it was early morning things were so quiet.

I found what looked like a place to eat. There was no closed sign, but the door appeared locked when I tried it. From inside there was a man's voice, "Give it a good kick!" With more of a push the door opened right up. Inside I could see the place was just a little country store where the owners lived too.

I asked, "Is this a restaurant?"

The man standing with a coffee cup in his hand looked like the owner. "Yep. This is the only one in Brownville."

"What you got for breakfast?"

The woman by the grill was probably his wife. She pointed to the board hanging on the wall with the hand-printed selections. "Anything up there."

"Well how about a stack of pancakes and bacon?"

"Sorry, we're out of pancake mix and bacon."

"Ok, how about some ..."

"Sorry, we're out of that too."

"Hmm. What do you have?"

"I can fix you an egg, ham and cheese on an English muffin."

"Fine. I'll have two."

It was like I was eating in the familiy's kitchen. She cooked from a small grill and there was just one table. The coffee really tasted good. We visited while the eggs took shape and the ham warmed. I told them about my trip and the man said that there was usually a canoe through here every one or two years. That matched with about what everyone else told me. Obviously this route wasn't a haven for people canoeing.

The breakfast sandwiches tasted great and these folks were certainly pleasant. They told me that there was a point of interest outside of town that I should visit. It was about 1-1/2 miles away and a bit of a climb, but from that high point you could see four states; Nebraska, Iowa, Kansas and Missouri. I thanked them for breakfast and said good-bye. All those states I would see from the river anyway. I really didn't feel like a walk and climb this morning. There was a small park with restrooms where I had left the canoe. I cleaned up, shaved and brushed my teeth before starting off again.

I was at least two days ahead of schedule. The river speed was predictable and with the mile markers along the way, I knew exactly how far I had to go to St. Louis. There was still three weeks left to my trip and I wanted it to be enjoyable. I would take my time now and be a tourist.

Folks had told me about some Indian caves close to the river. I didn't know exactly where they were and of course, unlike a highway, there were no informational signs along the way.

Just after a bend in the river I heard voices onshore and decided that maybe this was the area where the caves were at. There was a fast current making the landing a bit tricky, but I brought her in out of the fast water next to a fallen tree limb.

There were some people there watching me come in. They confirmed that the caves were only a short walk away. It was a really pretty area. A boardwalk went uphill through a thick canopy of hardwoods to a small pavilion. It was only a 10-minute walk.

The caves were located in a limestone cliff. One was about 20 feet in width and 6 to 8 feet high. People visiting had scratched their names on the walls. It looked tacky.

There were side trails off the boardwalk along the steep cliff. I had to carry a stick to clear out the spiders and webs that crossed the trail I was on. This trail led to a cave opening, which was about three feet wide. I could see tracks going in. It looked like I would be getting a little dirty, but I decided to go in anyway. The batteries in my little flashlight were almost dead. About 40 feet in I was developing this claustrophobic feeling. The ceiling was getting lower and lower. My knees and shoe tips were in wet clay as I crawled along. My back was starting to touch the damp ceiling. Around a little bend it got really dark. At best, I could only see five feet ahead. It seemed like a good time for retreat. Unfortunately there was no turning around. I had the flashlight in my mouth, but it was about useless so I put it back in the holster and started backing out on my hands and knees. There was only a thread of light behind me. I was nervous. Eventually, with skinned knees and muddy clothes, I emerged from the hole. There were some kids at the entrance watching as I tried to brush myself off. I told them there was nothing in there worth seeing. I'm not sure they were convinced.

Kansas was on the west side of the river. St. Joseph, Missouri, was the next big town and Kansas City not far beyond that. I wanted to get into St. Joseph early so that I could get a nice meal. More and more I was looking forward to something besides Ramen Noodles to eat.

St. Joseph seemed like a hustle and bustle city. A triple decker highway bridge crossed the river and I could see a couple of casino boats. One-and-a-half-foot waves were coming up the river to meet me and there didn't seem to be a good place to pull out. People on the deck of one casino boat were pointing at me. I waved and they waved back. Even the captain in the wheelhouse waved. I came closer and hollered up, "Anybody know where I can pull out of the river?" Nobody knew of anyplace. There were uninviting rocky retaining walls on both sides of the river.

On the southern side of the city I found what looked like a small creek entering the river. I paddled up that in hopes of finding a park or a place to hide the canoe. About a half-mile up this creek the smell of sewage got stronger and stronger. A thick scum was forming at the waterline on the canoe. It became apparent that I was on a waste water treatment outlet so I reversed course.

Back on the river I stayed close to shore as the wind had picked up. A motorboat with six guys in it was passing me by and they were all waving. I tried to motion them over, but they just waved some more. Finally they got the idea I wanted to talk to them and turned back.

"Hey, I'm looking for a place to pull out so I can get some dinner."

"There's nothing around here. You're welcome to come down to our fishing camp if you like. It's about five miles down."

They gave me directions and said they'd be back later after stocking up with beer.

Not far from a large highway bridge was a big yacht club. I didn't figure I'd be welcome there. Continuing down river, I spotted a small boat ramp poking out into the water. Up the hill from the ramp were some shade trees, an old school bus, two trailers and a couple of junk cars. Didn't look like much of a fishing camp, but must be the place. There also was a small pavilion with a barbecue grill.

A TV was on in one of the trailers. I knocked on the door. The camp proprietor came out. I told him that I had talked to some fishermen who said that possibly I could camp there tonight.

He said, "Yeah, sure. You look hot and tired; come on in." He dragged out two ice-cold beers. We talked a little about my trip, then he told about his fishing camp.

"I really need to get some groceries and something to eat. Can you give me some directions?"

"You pull your canoe in and I'll get my truck keys. I'll take you."

He drove me to Taco Bell and I wolfed down a bunch of soft tacos. We stopped by a small store and I picked up a few things, then returned to the camp.

We sat at a picnic table drinking another beer when the boatload of fishermen returned. They were pretty well trashed and not real couth. When they found out about my trip they had lots of questions. I wasn't in much of a conversational mood, especially with the condition these guys were in after drinking all day.

"I think I'm going to do some unpacking and relax. I'll meet you fellows out here a little later." I wasn't sure I would do that.

The camp owner suggested I sleep in the school bus. He said it belonged to Charlie, who wasn't here tonight and wouldn't mind. I thanked him and retrieved my bedroll from the canoe.

It was about dark out now. The school bus door was open. As I started through the opening I walked straight into a spider web. The web was wrapped around my face and the dime-sized occupant was there too. Quickly I wiped the web from my face, but it didn't feel like I got all of it off. The scene really grossed me out.

Inside I could hardly see where I was going. Finally I found a lamp and switched it on. Seconds after I clicked it on, the bulb burned out and I was in the dark again. In those few seconds of light I could easily determine that Charlie's retreat was not a picture of cleanliness. Dark, dingy, cluttered and musty smelling would be an accurate description. Oh well, I shouldn't bitch. I'll make the best of it, I thought. The bed was in the rear with an old mattress on it. I just laid my stuff right on the top. Didn't think I'd open it up.

When I went back to the pavilion the boys were all seated within close proximity to the ice chest full of beer. A couple of them were real weirdos. One offered me a pack of cigarettes and when I said, "No thanks," he got rather belligerent. Another told him to lay off. They were a rough-looking bunch too.

One of the group was the camp owner's son. He was around 30 years old and weighed about 300 pounds. He said that he was a diabetic, but he was putting away as much beer as the others. I told him my sister, Jeanne, was a diabetic too and we talked about that for awhile. Being the only sober person in this group, I could not honestly say I enjoyed the evening very much. I did appreciate their hospitality however, so I stayed for two or three hours, then excused myself.

As I reentered the school bus I walked right back into the spider web. It was unbelievable that in such a short period of time the spider could have restrung his web, but he sure did and he was still in there working. And he was probably just as pissed at me, for twice ruining his work, as I was mad at myself for walking into it again.

I plopped down on top of my bedroll and tried to sleep. It was just too hot. There was a back door, and when I opened that a nice breeze came through making things much more comfortable.

Up before light, I cooked a big bunch of french toast by the picnic table. The owner was around and invited me over for coffee before I left. I took my thermos with me and he filled it.

I thanked him for letting me stay there, and the use of Charlie's bus.

Atchison, Kansas, was an enjoyable stop. There was some kind of festival going on with lots of craft and food stands. While my dirty clothes were in the machine at the laundromat, I roamed around and sampled a few of the dessert delicacies.

I learned that Atchison was the hometown of the famed aviator Amelia Earhart. As a tribute to her, there are three big spotlights mounted on the bridge that crosses the Missouri. Each night they are turned on to guide her back home from wherever she might be.

Down at the river that evening, I visited with a gentleman who had purchased 20 acres of prime river property for only twenty thousand dollars. The only problem with the property was that it was a contaminated industrial site. His plan was to excavate the top three feet of soil and replace it with clean soil, then develop or sell the land for a big profit. That sounded like quite an undertaking, but it was a nice piece of property.

After Atchison the river current really slowed down. There were lots of sand bar islands covered with cattails. In the distance I could see some guys with machetes chopping down the cattails and putting them in their boat. I never heard of anyone harvesting cattails before. What I should have done was paddle over and see what they were up to, but I just kept going. Later on I did discover that the cattails were tied into bundles and used to camouflage goose hunting blinds.

The geese blinds were pretty neat. These box-like hutches were four to five feet tall and long enough to pull a boat into. The outside was covered with bundles of cattails and the top could be moved off to allow for shooting. There were lots of hunters in camouflage gear all along this stretch of river. The season must have been just getting underway. A couple of them sounded their goose calls when they saw me gliding by. I'll bet one guy had at least 150 decoys around his blind.

The next town of dubious fame is Leavenworth, home of the military's hard-core criminals. I'll bet the boys up there busting rocks would be happy to trade places with me. If they'd let me in I'd give a little lecture to the clientele. I doubt I'd be welcome as I've heard entertainment is not part of the curriculum there. I was a little curious to see what the place looked like but decided to drift by and just be able to say I'd passed near it.

The Kansas City radio stations kept talking about a renaissance festival taking place not far from the city. A year ago when I visited my brother Clark in Tucson, I borrowed his motorcycle and rode to one and it was really interesting. People were dressed in medieval costumes and there were jousting contests, sword fights and all sort of activities. What a great way to spend a day on the Missouri. I just had to find out where it was.

There was a jogging path along the river for a ways, so when someone came along I'd back paddle and ask if they knew where the renaissance festival was taking place. They had heard of it too, but didn't know any details.

On the left side of the river was a fancy boat marina. I cut out of the swift current and maneuvered through some boats to tie the canoe off at a gangplank. There was an old guy onshore sitting on a rock. The man reminded me of Uncle Jessie from The Dukes of Hazzard TV show. He had a long white beard and sideburns and was real friendly, but didn't know anything about the festival. He went over and asked a boat mechanic.

"The mechanic says it's about 20 miles from the Missouri. How you going to get out there?"

I answered, "Well, I'll hitchhike maybe. Someway I'll find some transportation."

"You could paddle up the Kansas River. The river goes right through the festival area."

"Why not, I have a couple days to kill," I said.

Kansas City is a big rail hub and my path took me by a huge rail yard in addition to the large airport. There were lots of bridges over the river all through town. Right in downtown the river makes a sharp bend to the east. At that point the Kansas River joins from the west. I continued straight past the bend into the Kansas.

On the outskirts of town I stopped to ask directions from a black fisherman named Larry. Like a lot of people who have spent most of their lives in a city, miles don't mean much, it's the amount of time that they judge distance by. From what I could tell by Larry's time estimate I had 15 to 20 miles to paddle against a 2 mph current. It certainly would be a lot of extra work, but I was sure the festival would be worth it. Before I left I had a nice visit with Larry. He wanted to know about my trip and I wanted to know what kind of fish he was after. Larry pulled up a string of fish which included two 20 to 30 pound channel catfish and a couple of big buffalo carp.

It was lunchtime. I tied off at a dock and climbed a steep hill to see where I was. Just over the crest of the hill I almost bumped into this guy in a 2-piece suit. We both were surprised with the other's presence. He seemed nervous. I asked him for directions to a fast food restaurant. He looked at me funny and said he didn't know and walked off. Kind of a weird guy. I wondered where in the world he came from dressed like that. I'm sure he wondered where the river rat came from too. I hadn't shaved lately and probably looked a bit rough.

My peanut butter and jelly sandwich was ready and I just started chomping away when down to the dock came six very cute girls in shorts carrying a small rowboat. Even though they were of high school age they sure were a pleasant sight for sore eyes. They went back and crossed paths with girls carrying another boat and paddles down. This went on until they had about 10 of these solo rowboats or sculls and a small motorboat onshore. They gave me the once-over, but went about their business. Curiosity got the best of me and I went over and asked them what was going on. I was told that this group was the local high school rowing team. They routinely row up river for five miles, go around an island and come back downstream. The motorboat was for the coach and two guys that helped out.

Finally the coach arrived. He was the guy in the two-piece suit I almost bumped into.

I left ahead of the girls and waited a half-mile ahead. They were all facing downstream rowing, so as they passed I paddled along and had no problem keeping up with their pace. As they rowed around the island to start back downstream I waved good-bye and continued on.

Along the riverbank there were lots of fishing lines hanging down from the trees. Also there were some floating milk jugs which probably marked the position of some nets. I pulled up one line and on the end was a large goldfish hooked through the tail. That's what they were using for bait.

Further up I gave another line a tug. It felt like it was hooked onto a log. I detected some movement in the line. Another pull and I could tell there was a fish on it. After I wrapped the line around my hand I started to pull whatever was hooked through the murky water to the surface. This had to be one friggin' big fish. It didn't take much more pull until I was face to face with the biggest catfish I had ever seen. His head was as big as a basketball, with a big old set of whiskers. I had him almost out of the water when all of a sudden he kicks in with that big old tail and totally drenches me. That I was not prepared for. Needless to say, he went back in the water and I wiped my face off.

I don't think I had made more than a dozen strokes with the paddle, when from this large hole in the embankment came the biggest beaver I had ever seen. He splashed into the water five feet away and dove under my canoe. The catfish and the beaver incident all happened within a couple of minutes of each other and my heart rate was all pumped up. I passed a fisherman and asked how far it was to the bridge where I would be getting out. He wasn't sure, but he did say that there was a big rock dam ahead that I couldn't go around.

It was getting dark when I reached the dam. It did look formidable. The rocks sloped up to a 10 foot height and when I climbed to the top I could see that the rocks continued on the other side for 100 feet. It was a lot of work just climbing over these boulders to the top.

I would have preferred to be on the other side of the rocks before morning. It was too late though. I started my cooking water boiling and laid out the bedroll.

With a full stomach of mashed potatoes, stove top dressing and sardines, I laid back and listened to the water cascading through the rocks. What a pleasant soothing sound it was. I dreaded carrying all my stuff over the rocks in the morning. The festival shouldn't be too much further away. I hoped it was a good one.

In the morning it took six trips to get everything on the other side of the dam. Upstream from the dam I came upon an operating sand dredge. At first it looked stationary, but then I could detect a slight movement. The Captain came out on deck to say hello. I told him what I was doing and that I was curious about his operation. "Come on up to my boathouse, I'll show you around," he said.

The sand dredge moved about a foot every five minutes. Huge diesel generators ran motors that created the vacuum to suck the sand up into a hose. A giant blade held a very slow-moving chain conveyor into the river bottom to dig it up for the vacuum. He showed me all the controls. It was a one-man operation which sure looked boring.

The river became very shallow. I tried to stay in the main channel but was continually getting stuck on sand bars. Two miles short of my goal I had enough. There was a big hill and beyond that a sand mining company. Earlier I had paddled past the sand dredge and here the sand was being processed. Conveyors were transporting the sand to shakers and separators. Everything was running full tilt. I walked up to the control room and through the partially open door could see the operator was on the phone. I stayed out by the door until he hung up and then I introduced myself. I told him I was ahead of schedule canoeing the Missouri, and thought I'd spend a day at the renaissance festival.

"Gee, the festival is only on weekends," he said.

"No, that can't be right. Several people have told me it's going on right now," I responded.

"Well, come on in. I'll call city hall and find out."

The office was air-conditioned, which was a relief from the heat. He looked through the phone book, then dialed a number and asked the responder about the festival. When he hung up he said, "Sorry, the festival is only on the weekends. It was now the first of the week and I had just missed it. Bummer. All this way just to turn around and go back over that dam. I was really disappointed.

Before I left the sand processing facility I told the man about my trip and then he escorted me around to explain his operation. That tour wasn't quite what I had in mind to come this far, but I enjoyed it just the same.

Going back down over the dam took almost as long as it had going up in the morning. Finally I had everything across, rested and ate lunch. I wanted to make Kansas City again before dark. There wasn't much current, so I knew it would take awhile. At least the water was fairly deep and I wouldn't have to contend with the sand bars.

Back in Kansas City I started passing under the big bridges again. They were all real high to allow for the river barges to pass underneath. I received several tips from people along the way recommending that I not camp in certain areas along the river. I was hungry though, and dirty and stinky. At one of the last bridges I saw a casino sign advertising a dinner special. I stopped and took a sponge bath under the bridge. Anyone passing overhead might see the canoe, but not me. After a shave I put on some clean clothes and headed to the casino for supper.

The casino security guards gave me a player's courtesy card which allowed me two dollars in tokens or that much off the price of the buffet. For eight dollars I had a fantastic meal; steak, lasagna, Mexican food. They had it all and I loaded right up. I walked back to the bridge with my empty water jugs. I had forgotten to get them filled. Oh well, there would be someplace downstream to do it.

Arriving back at the bridge my canoe was not up on the boulders where I left it. It was out in the river and would have been miles down river had I not tied it securely. Apparently a barge went by and washed it off the rocks. Boy was I lucky. I learned a valuable lesson. Next time I must pull the old Bell way up onshore or risk losing her.

It was starting to get dark out and I needed some water before picking out my campsite for the evening. Another river casino boat was alongshore. I thought I'd try that. People were on deck watching as I approached in the fast current. I yelled up to one of the security guards, "How's chances of getting my water jugs filled?"

"No problem. Come around to the back entrance."

The back entrance took me right into a group of pretty girls that were getting their costumes adjusted for a show dance routine. I had to snake my way through the girls to the kitchen, to get my jugs filled. I don't think they enjoyed the intrusion but I did.

Back on the river, there was a big celebration this evening. One of the old paddle-wheel river boats that had been in Kansas City for many years had been purchased and was on her last run before she went down the rivers to Florida. It was a gigantic party with fireworks and everything, all just ahead of me.

I found a nice sandy beach and decided to call it a day. It was dark out now. I pulled the canoe way up onshore. There was a grassy area to hide it and a good place for my bedroll too. A sign gave directions to another casino off the river. I took a path through the weeds for a half-mile and finally found it. To be a legal gambling establishment the place had to be on a boat on the Missouri or technically Missouri River water. What they did was dig a big pond and fill it with water from the river, then build their casino on a barge floating in the pond. The pond and river boat were both completely enclosed in a huge building. On the land around the pond they had assembled what looked like an old western town with a boardwalk and numerous shops. The ceiling to the building that housed all this was painted blue so that you had the impression you were still outdoors.

I walked around and peeked in the shops, then looked for a phone to call home. There were some phones, but I needed a calling card and they didn't sell them here. I left the place and walked a couple miles to a gas station where I could buy one. I talked with Renae, Mom and Mary Ann. I told them that I was in Kansas City and things were going well except for my aborted trip to the renaissance festival.

It was almost 1 a.m. when I curled up in my sleeping bag. What a full day it had been.

Missouri

October 8th to October 12th

The rest of my trip would take me from the west side of Missouri, bordering Kansas, to the far east side next to Illinois. Before the sun came up, I had a mini breakfast of orange juice and cinnamon rolls that I had purchased at a gas station the previous night. It was a good night's sleep and I was ready for the day.

According to my map, the little town of Napoleon looked like it would make a good lunch stop; it was about 25 miles from my morning start point. I almost canoed past the town, as it was much smaller than I expected. The main street only had a couple of stores.

A lady in the deli made me a nice sandwich and then I wandered around in a small antique shop. A couple of older folks owned the shop and I had a nice visit with them. They told me that a hundred or so years ago the river course was a half-mile further north. There was a big storm one day and a river boat ran into some rocks in that area. The people on board got out safely, but the boat sank. Apparently it was traveling upstream at the time and filled with cargo.

Over the years, the river altered its course and the boat was covered with silt and buried in what became a flood plain. In recent years two partners decided they would excavate the site and dig out the old river boat, with its cargo. Even though the boat was a quarter of a mile from the river, each time they tried to dig around it the hole would fill with water and cave in. Finally they decided to work at it when it was cold enough for their hole to stay frozen. I didn't see the site, but I guess from what the folks said the two men were making reasonable progress and from the back window of the antique shop you could see the crane they were using.

My plan was to spend the evening in Lexington. According to the map there was an historical site there. It was sprinkling that afternoon so I traveled with my rain gear on.

When I approached the city, it was still raining lightly. There didn't seem to be any kind of boat landing. I did find a small creek or, really, just a ditch that led in the direction of the city. Following that, I ended up behind a water treatment facility. It was a hassle getting the canoe out of the ditch because the grassy clay bank was really slippery from the rain.

There didn't seem to be any good place to set up camp. The rain stopped for awhile, so I decided to clean up, leave the canoe, and find someplace in town to spend the night. I was in dire need of a good bath. Down at the river I worked my way out on a dead log past the soft clay and lowered myself into the river. After a good scrubbing, I toweled off and made my way back along the log. Eventually I still had to walk back through the muck as my clothes were back by the canoe. I sat down, rinsed my feet off again with some drinking water, and put clean clothes on.

Here again the river had changed its course over time. I had to walk across this flood plain, which was full of brush, to get up the hillside to where the city started. I packed a bag with my bedroll, my mattress and a few things I needed for the night, then buttoned up the canoe. The waist high foliage was all wet so I put my rain gear back on for the walk through it.

There was a truck at the water treatment facility. I knocked on the office door, but there was no answer. I was about to leave when a gentleman opened the door. He was the sole employee here and seemed quite friendly, inviting me in. I told him what I was doing and that I was curious how his facility operated. My interest in his work seemed to please him. He gave me a nice tour and explanation on how the water was purified. It involved several tanks where different chemicals were added. One additive, I believe, was iron sulfate. Somehow it attached to particles in the water and turned it to a rust color. A neutralizer was then added in another tank and that caused the contaminants to precipitate to the bottom. The end result of this process was good water for Lexington. Before leaving I asked if he thought my canoe would be safe in back of the plant. He said that as long as it was raining out, he didn't expect anyone would be wandering down here. He thought my stuff would be OK. I thanked him, grabbed my bag, then walked through the wet lowland leaves again and up the hill to town.

It was obvious that Lexington was a rather old town, but the buildings and everything were really well cared for. I found my way to the library and by that time it was sprinkling again. The librarian was pleasant enough and gave me information on points of interest, plus the location of some restaurants in town. She even allowed me to leave my stuff behind her desk while I toured.

Lexington was the site of a civil war battle and the tall brick courthouse was where the defenders were finally able to hold off the enemy. It was a fall back position, and they surrounded the building with bales of hemp. Hemp was being grown to make rope out of, not for smoking. They poured water on the bales of hemp which gave them density enough to stop bullets and not burn. The bales proved to be a formidable barrier. The enemy, however, did set up a cannon on a near hill and lobbed balls into the courthouse area. One ball lodged into the upper part of one of the big white pillars in front. It remained there for many years after the war until eventually it fell out. They put that ball in the local museum, but placed another one back up in the hole permanently, for it had become quite a tourist attraction.

I had a nice dinner and spent some more time reading at the library. I heard there was a place to camp in a park pavilion some distance away. The library closed at 8 p.m., so I picked up my stuff and half-heartedly headed in the direction of the park. With all the exercise that day, a closer place to camp would be much better than a long walk in the dark.

Off on the grass, someone had a large pickup truck camper top with a for sale sign on it. That might be a nice dry place for the night. I lifted the back door and pushed my bag in. I crawled underneath, inflated my mattress and spread the bedroll out. There wasn't much room, but it was dry and quite cozy. With the flashlight in my mouth I sat down and wrote a single letter home.

That night it started raining again. The raindrops made plenty of noise on the fiberglass camper top, but I was warm, dry and comfortable inside; I didn't care.

When I woke up it was still dark out. After a quick glance at my watch, I told myself it was about 6 a.m. and time to get going. It did seem like a rather short night. After deflating my mattress, I put everything in the bag and walked up to the restaurant for breakfast. There was a closed sign on the door. I thought that was funny. The place was supposed to be open by now. Another closer look at my watch revealed that it was really 2 a.m. No wonder it seemed like such a short night. I went back, inflated my mattress and slept four more hours.

The next time I showed up the restaurant was open. I ordered breakfast and while my meal was being prepared I read the paper and had a cup of coffee. There were some elderly people at a nearby table. They were talking about some guy canoeing down the river that had been over at the library. Eventually a man came over to ask me something and in short order word was out that I was the stranger in town. The questions started coming about the same time as my breakfast. In between mouthfuls of food I tried to courteously carry on a conversation.

The library had a computer, so I spent some time on the internet. Next I visited the museum, toured a battlefield and just wandered around enough to get a good feel for the town.

I arrived out at the little park about 6:30 p.m. I put my gear in the pavilion and looked around for something to do until bedtime. There was a boy scout meeting hall bordering the park. A truck pulled up to the building and an older man went inside. I ambled over and thought maybe I could strike up a conversation. I knocked on the door and he hollered, "Come on in."

There were several tables inside all covered with spread-out tents. The man that just arrived sat at a desk at the front of the room and was shuffling through some papers. I introduced myself and told him that because of the rain I was taking a couple of days off from my trip and was touring Lexington. He asked several questions about my trip and as I talked he leaned back in the swivel chair with his hands clasped behind his head. An unlit cigar protruded from the side of his mouth; he bit down on it and started to grin.

"What are you doing tonight?" he asked.

"Nothing special. My bedroll is out in the pavilion. I'm sleeping there tonight, leaving tomorrow morning."

"We're having a scout meeting tonight at eight. I wondered what I was going to talk about. Would you do a little presentation?"

"Sure, I'd be happy to."

A couple of the other scout leaders arrived early. From them I learned a little about the Lexington Boy Scout troop, which happened to be one of the oldest in the nation. There seemed to be plenty of community support for the scout program here and the boys took a lot of pride in their membership. Many of them even wore their scout merit badges to school.

As the boys trickled in they gave me a curious glance, but soon were busy folding up the tents that had been airing out from the previous week's camping trip. I noticed that each boy wore a necklace with what looked like a varying amount of bear claws hanging from it. I was told that these were Indian theme merits. Each claw represented a different accomplishment. Just before 8 p.m., about 20 more kids came in, along with a few fathers who were staying for the meeting. The man I first talked with moved up to the podium and rapped his gavel to get everyone's attention.

"Take your seats, boys, and quiet down. You guys are really lucky tonight. This young man just walked in the door and I think what he's doing is really neat." He went on with this nice introduction and I thought to myself, I hope I can live up to this guy's expectations. There were a total of about 30 scouts, 5 or 6 fathers, plus the leaders, and I was a tad bit nervous.

"I'm Scott Galloway from Michigan. I am canoeing the Yellowstone and Missouri Rivers from Billings, Montana to St. Louis, Missouri; about 2400 miles altogether." I told them that I had been in the cub scouts when I was young and wished that I had been a boy scout as they were. After spending 10 minutes generalizing about my trip I asked for questions. I swear, every hand went up.

After 1-1/2 hours of answering questions, I had to ask for a glass of water because my voice was getting raspy from talking so much. Finally I took the last question from kind of a punky looking boy in the front row. He seemed a bit timid. It was his first question.

"Why are you doing this, to be famous?"

I had been asked this before, and it was my favorite question to answer.

"I'm doing this because I'm young and single, in good physical condition, and for me it is a neat challenging adventure. This trip will also give me some nice stories to tell my grandkids."

"No, I'm not doing this to be famous, but I do enjoy telling people about my trip. Sometimes those people are TV and newspaper reporters; in fact there may be something about my trip in your newspaper. These reporters don't come to me because I'm famous, they come and ask questions because they think their readers will be interested in what I'm doing."

One of the fathers in the back of the room raised his hand, then stood up and started talking. "I got goose bumps when you told your story. I'm married with kids and I've never done anything big like that. I think you're doing this trip for all the right reasons. I admire you for dropping your work and pursuing something like this."

I responded, "Thank you. That makes me feel good. You know, when people come and ask about my trip, after I tell them then they will share with me something big that happened in their lives. So you see, this adventure is a learning experience for me too. I find out about other people, their adventures and a big part of all of this is hearing about the history along the river."

Concluding, I said, "If you put your mind to it, you can have your own adventure. Maybe it will be backpacking, a hunting trip or something else, but you can do it. I've really enjoyed talking to you all. Thank you."

There was a standing ovation and I felt a twinge of embarrassment.

It was almost 10 p.m. and I think the meeting might have run longer than usual. Parents were waiting outside and it wasn't long before the place emptied out. One of the leaders offered to have me stay at his place for the night, but I thanked him and declined.

I guess I was still a little keyed up from the evening's activities, because I certainly wasn't sleepy. I wandered around town and looked at the old homes that were so nicely preserved. I thought about the scouts. They sure were a fine bunch of boys. Their questions were excellent and they were attentive to what I had to say. I hoped they learned something from me.

There was an old man sitting and enjoying a cigarette on the porch of a retirement home. I asked if he minded if I joined him for a few minutes. We had a good conversation and it was a pleasant way to end this nice evening before I turned in.

About 2 a.m. I woke up to a violent storm. Rain was coming down in sheets and it entered the pavilion at a threatening angle. A large puddle was working its way towards my sleeping bag. My clothes, left out, were already wet so I crawled out of the sleeping bag in my underwear and moved over behind the fireplace. That offered some shelter from the howling wind. Soon I was back to sleep.

It was clear and sunny the next morning. I pushed my way through the brush on the flood plain and even though the canoe was right where I left it, the place was a greasy, muddy mess. I had a heck of a time getting the canoe down to the stream. My hiking boots were covered with mud.

I paddled almost 60 miles that day. Waverly was the only town close to the river and I stopped there at a small cafe for lunch. At dark I arrived near a park outside of Miami. The place was empty. After hiding the canoe, I walked through town and asked a man if there was a restaurant close by. There was just one and it was a mile or so away. That too was empty, so I had a beer and ate my dinner in peace. Walking back through town, it seemed as if there was an unusual amount of dogs barking and running loose. Fortunately they didn't bother me or come down to the park. It was a pretty night and I slept under a big willow tree right beside the river.

Up early, I had a quick pop tart breakfast with juice. I would stop at Glasgow for a good meal and some supplies.

Glasgow was an old river boat town. Originally built close to the river, the town had been flooded and in later years was moved to higher ground. They were having sidewalk sales that day, so a lot of people were in town shopping. At a recommended restaurant, I had a Reuben sandwich and visited with a nice elderly couple. I picked up a few supplies and ambled around town, looking at the historic buildings. In this part of town there was a boardwalk instead of a cement sidewalk. On one of the buildings, a man of retirement age was high up on a ladder tuck pointing. That's the process of replacing the mortar between the old building stones, which is exactly what I do for a living with D.C. Byers in Grand Rapids.

I yelled up to him, "Hey, that's what I do for a living."

He looked down with a grin, "Well ya sure can't find anyone around here to do this kind of work."

He came down the ladder and explained that this was the old newspaper building that they were fixing up. I hadn't recognized it as the newspaper office, but once this gentleman found out what I was doing he asked me to wait and soon had a reporter out talking to me. The reporter went back in for a pencil and paper and I was sitting on a bench answering the usual questions. He took a picture of me and the old guy.

I spotted a tug pushing six barges up the river. My canoe was only 10 feet or so up onshore, so I quickly bought a local newspaper, grabbed my supplies and hurried back down to pull the canoe farther away from the river. The tugboat captain waved. I read over the newspaper until the barges were well past, then started my journey again.

In my haste to get down to the waterfront before the barges passed, I had neglected one of my morning duties. Just on the outskirts of town, I pulled over to find a private spot to relieve my bladder. I pulled the canoe up on the sandy beach, climbed up the embankment and stepped into the trees. As I stood there I could hear a male turkey in the woods. He didn't sound far away. From under the canoe cover I retrieved my gun and a few 22 shells. I knew that I would have trouble bringing down a big turkey with the shotgun.

Slowly and quietly I made my way through the woods to where I had last heard the gobbler. I came to an area where the brush and vines combined to make any further movement forward very difficult. If I tried to push through, I would create so much noise he would be long gone. His calls came fairly regularly, but they seemed to be getting further away. I did my best to mimic his call a couple of times. There was silence for a few moments, then he answered. It was the first time I had even tried to call a turkey, but apparently he liked what he heard. He was moving towards my position. Turkeys have eyesight like hawks and I knew the slightest movement would spook him.

From behind a clump of vines he came into view. His feathers were not up so he probably thought I was another male. His waddles were very large and hung down like a long beard. I had my sights on him. He was well within range and I knew that the 22 magnum could bring him down if my shot was true. What bothered me was that I was still close to town. I would have to drag him down to the beach to dress him out, and someone might see me and not appreciate the stranger harvesting their turkeys. Or, maybe I just liked seeing this old bird strutting around and decided to spare him. I turned ever so slowly just to see if he would notice. In an instant he was on his way deeper into the woods.

Fifteen miles north of Boonville there is a place called Boons Lick. There the pioneers discovered caves with salty mineral water bubbling out. They brought in big cast-iron pots to boil the water away and collect the salt. For several years it was a thriving business and the big iron kettles are still there for people to see.

The city of Boonville, like most river towns, is built up on the high ground. I found a small park and pavilion on the outskirts of town; it was around 7 p.m. There is a nice pedestrian walkway on the bridge over the Missouri. I stopped in the center and just sat down for several minutes enjoying the view.

The concrete where I sat was still warm. The sun had already set and the western horizon was aglow with its radiance. Another fellow walked by and I said, "Nice sunset, huh?" He sat down and we talked for awhile.

Near the river I saw a black man, his wife and little girl tending some fishing lines. I said hello and asked questions about his fishing. He said a license only cost two dollars and you were allowed to have 24 lines within a certain distance; 500 feet, I believe. His wire fishing lines were attached to metal stakes in the embankment and were baited with slightly aged, smelly, goldfish. As the man pulled up a fish his little girl would be right there with a net to capture it. Some he kept, some he threw back. He did have about 5 nice big catfish.

The fisherman's name was Leo. His wife and daughter were very pleasant and I like Leo, but he had this chip on his shoulder about white people and kept making little cutting remarks. I told him that we were planning to write a small book about my river trip and that I would be sure to put something in there about him and his nice family. Leo's answer to this was, "Yeah, you can put in there that we were the Black family that didn't rob ya."

"Leo, you got to let it go and get past this thing."

"I was just kidding," he said. I knew that some experience in the past had made him feel bitter and his remarks weren't just accidental. I still liked this guy and had him pose for a picture. I told him maybe I'd see him in the morning.

It was a two-mile walk to the restaurant that night, but it was worth it. A great meal in a nice old-time room with high ceilings. The only problem was that when I arrived back at the camp, I remembered I had left my glasses on the table at the restaurant. After going back for my glasses I had logged eight miles of walking and was ready for the sack. That night it seemed like trains went by every half-hour and the place just shook. After awhile I became accustomed to the noise and still had a good sleep.

Before I left the next morning I wrote a note to Leo. I told him what a great family he had and that I had enjoyed meeting him. After folding the note, I put LEO in large block letters on the outside and tied it to one of his fish line stakes. I made up a nice batch of french toast and ate on a picnic table. There was a light drizzle, so after packing up the canoe I put on my rain gear. The rain continued, increasing in intensity. I tightened the canoe cover around my waist. There was no wind and I was dry. If it didn't get any worse then this I could continue. It did get worse and after 25 miles I had enough. I started looking for shelter, ending up under a bridge. The rain came down even heavier. I needed a better place to camp than this. Further past the bridge there was a small creek outlet and I knew not too far up that stream a railroad bridge crossed. Perhaps I could find shelter there.

The rain let up for a short period and I spotted some ducks. I retrieved my gun from under the cover and nailed one with my first shot. Nearing the train trestle I could see that it would offer little protection if it started raining again. As I turned the canoe back downstream, something caught my eye from the cliff above; a roof of some sort. I pulled out and stepped into a gush of mud. Collecting some sticks, I laid them down close enough together to keep me out of most of the mud.

Up on the creek embankment I found a 15x20 foot shingle roof mounted on posts. It looked like the shelter would offer good protection from the rain. Floods had washed enough silt into it to leave only about a four-foot-high space underneath. Nevertheless it was the best shelter available. I had very little water left, but enough to cook my duck with and maybe a half cup left over for drinking water.

I dressed the duck, quartered him and put him into boiling water with onions to simmer. With the canoe onshore I got my gear out and buttoned her up. It was still raining lightly. In the shelter I had to continuously bend over because of the roof height. At least it was dry and pretty much blocked the wind. There was a folding chair inside along with a rusty grill.

While the duck was simmering, I took the gun out to see if I could get anymore game. I didn't have any luck, so I took a look at the map to see where I could get some more gas for my stove. There were two towns fairly close. Lupus was the closest, but on the other side of the river. Huntsdale I could reach by walking down the railroad track. I liked the sound of that name better anyway. I decided to go there after dinner.

My dinner was very tasty, duck, mashed potatoes and soup. Fortunately the gas lasted until everything was cooked. I knew with only a little water left I would be thirsty before morning, but I thought the gas might be even more of a morale booster to have some hot food in the morning. Huntsdale was a long walk and I didn't feel like carrying both jugs.

With my raincoat on, I started down the tracks towards town. There were cornfields on both sides of the tracks and I noticed quite a few dead animals along the way. These tracks were quite shiny and, judging from all the trains I heard the previous night, they probably had quite a bit of traffic. The animals obviously tried to run down the tracks to get away from the trains and lost the race; an opossum here, then a skunk, even a turtle shell.

There were thunderstorms building in the west. I sure was glad I brought along my raincoat. It also was supposed to be chilly tonight so I put on a long sleeved shirt, sweat shirt and Levis.

Well, I walked and walked and finally reached Huntsdale. What a disappointment it was. There was no post office, gas station, party store, bar, no stores at all, just eight or nine houses. A guy was working under his car and I asked if there was anyplace near where I could get some gas.

"Sorry, you came to the wrong town, but I can give you a little gas," he said.

"Well, that's what I came for. If you can help me out that's all I need."

I offered several times, but he wouldn't take pay for the gas. Back down the tracks I had five miles to get back to camp. The thunderstorm looked much closer.

The wind really started to pick up as the storm moved overhead. Every time I faced down the tracks my hood blew off. Soon it started raining some, then more and more. Now it was a heavy rain and my blue jeans were soaked. I tried to walk sideways down the tracks to keep my face out of the wind and the rain which was pelting me. I was grumbling about how miserable I was and then I heard the train whistle. Turning around, I could see the big coal train would be on me in seconds. I leaped off the tracks and it roared by at about 50 mph. The rain had made so much noise on my hood I hadn't heard it coming. If the engineer hadn't seen me and blown the whistle, I'd be lying there right along next to the other dead animals that had fallen prey to the iron monster. I don't know how the engineer saw me. My rain jacket was a dark color as were my blue jeans. It was still a little light out, so I wouldn't have shown up in the train's light very well. Thank God that man was vigilant and sounded his whistle. It sure scared the hell out of me but saved my life. I just stood there shaking and stunned as the long coal train rattled past.

By the time I got back to the camp area it was dark. I had marked the area where I wanted to leave the tracks, but I couldn't find my mark. You can bet that every 30 seconds I was looking around for another train. Finally I left the tracks and ended up making my way back through a tangle of grapevines and underbrush. I thought to myself, "Things are really not going my way today."

After some healthy cursing, I finally found my way back to camp. I peeled off the wet clothes and put on some dry sweat pants and another shirt. The flashlight was in my mouth while I rummaged around in the dry food bag. Something fell off the rafters. It looked like an acorn. I reached down, picked it up and brought it close for examination in the beam of the flashlight. About the time I got it close to my face, it turned into a really nasty looking yellow spider with black spots. It had its legs tucked in when it fell and now it was spread out to full width. That fella sure gave me a scare and I tossed him out of my quarters.

Boy was I thirsty, but no water ... except that falling out of the sky onto my roof. I held out my jug and let some trickle in. I collected a half quart. That took quite awhile. Now I wished it would rain a little harder so I could get more faster. About 3 a.m. I got my wish. It poured and started blowing under the roof. After moving the sleeping bag to a dryer spot, I positioned my teakettle to catch some more water from the roof. It was full in no time at all. Back in my warm bedroll I mulled over the day's happenings. Everything worked out OK, but what an ordeal it had been. I thought that all the excitement of this trip was past, but now I began to wonder. Would there be more? I wouldn't have to wait long to find out.

The Hobo

October 13th to October 16th

With the morning light, I could see that the rain water I had collected from the roof looked rather milky. Probably leaves had collected on the roof and, as thirsty as I was, I wanted to make sure it was clean before I drank it. I skimmed off what I could see floating on top, then boiled it for five minutes.

The rain had stopped, but the trees around were still dripping. I cooked up a bunch of pancakes and finally got everything packed up by 9:30. It was a late start, but it had been a long night, too.

In Marion I stopped for lunch. Not far after that, when I came around a bend in the river, I saw in the distance the big white dome of the Jefferson City capitol building. I was still 10 or 15 miles away, but even at that distance the building was impressive.

As I came into the outskirts of Jefferson City, the state capitol building seemed even more imposing. With gray granite or limestone walls, it stood about seven stories high. It was just a beautiful building that dominated the city.

I began looking for a place to pull out. There was a large boat landing, but several kids were fishing there and I worried about the security of my gear. There seemed to be a lot of homeless folks down by the river, too.

A little creek entered the river and I followed that towards the city as far as I could go. It traveled through concrete tunnels and under several highway bridges. High concrete walls bordered the stream on both sides. A few inches up from the water level there were ledges in the walls and a lot of these were covered with vines. I thought one of the ledges would offer good concealment for the canoe while I toured the city. I put on some clean clothes, got some cash and pulled the canoe up on a ledge. I covered it with an army blanket, then spread the vines over all of it. Even at close range a person would have trouble seeing it.

I walked to the capitol building and again marveled at the architecture and the carvings that decorated it. I spent quite a bit of time touring the building and a museum on the bottom floor. By this time my pancakes had worn off and I was hungry again. A guide at the museum gave me directions to where the fast food restaurants were located. I found a Domino's Pizza, ordered a large one, and while they were preparing it I walked to a Baskin Robbins for a 44-ounce strawberry malt. My plan was to carry my food back to the canoe and slowly gorge myself.

My path to the canoe was near the expressway. I saw this guy coming down an exit ramp carrying a suitcase. He looked clean-cut and I figured he was hitchhiking through the area. As we passed I said, "You on the road too?" He stopped and turned around, "I've been living in Kentucky, but came down here looking for work."

"Are you hungry? I've got a large pizza here and I can't eat all of it by myself."

"Thanks anyway. The guy I was riding with just stopped at Wendy's."

There was a small pavilion on the capitol grounds where I sat down to devour my pizza and malt. It was a pleasant setting with fountains and numerous flower beds nearby. Police officers continually roamed the capitol grounds and, although they didn't bother me, it just wasn't a fitting place to hang out for a long period of time. With all the homeless folks around, I also was concerned about the security of my canoe.

I finished the pizza, but I was so full it was pathetic. The canoe was just as I had left it, but I decided to paddle on down past Jefferson City for the night. It was dusk when I entered the river again.

Ten or fifteen miles past Jefferson City the Osage River dumps in. It's getting late and I'm getting antsy to find a place for the night. There is a fairly high ridge on the south side of the river, but I couldn't see any boat docks. Finally I spotted a boat landing with a concrete driveway leading all the way up the steep incline of the ridge. That looked good enough. According to the radio it was to be down in the 30's tonight, so I spread a tarp across from the canoe to the road curb and put my air mattress and bedroll underneath.

At the top of the ridge I could see two compounds about a quarter of a mile apart with a high chain link and barbed wire fence going around. Trucks were driving back and forth across the area between and around the compounds.

During the night cold air seemed to float down the concrete driveway and end up right under my tarp. Even though I was buried in my sleeping bag, I shivered and was cold all night. Periodically trucks would come by and stop at the top of the ridge, but none came down, nor did they shine their spotlights on me. In the morning another look confirmed that this was some kind of prison location.

That morning I noticed a pretty little creek entering the Missouri. I had lots of time so I decided to paddle up it for a ways. An old rail bridge going over the stream had been converted to a pedestrian and bike path. The walkway led to a trail that followed the stream. The scenery was absolutely beautiful. A huge limestone cliff bordered one side. It was covered with ivy and water trickled down it to the river. The trees formed a canopy overhead, but still allowed some shafts of morning sunlight to come through. The water was so clear and smooth that it was almost mirrorlike in reflecting everything around it. I stopped paddling and laid back to listen to the trickling water. There seemed to be an abundance of happy chirping birds around. This was absolutely the most pleasant spot I had found since starting the trip. A half-mile upstream it became too shallow to paddle, so I turned around and let the little stream quickly take me back to the river. (The cover photo is from this area.)

After reentering the river I saw a john boat with a cabin on it anchored in the shade along the shoreline. When I got closer I could see men inside. The sign on the outside of the boat said something about river surveying. Five guys were inside eating lunch when I pulled alongside. I think I kind of surprised them. Introducing myself, I said it was about my lunchtime too and asked if they minded if I joined them. They were certainly a friendly bunch and were more than happy to have me climb on board.

For 1-1/2 hours we enjoyed our lunch and visited. They had lots of questions about my trip and I was curious about what they were up to. I learned that their work involved maintaining the finger dikes. I had seen lots of them coming down the river. These long narrow piles of boulders protruded out into the river and were positioned strategically to protect the shoreline from erosion. This was especially important around bridges. The dikes directed the force of the river out into the channel. During the winter, chunks of ice would loosen and move the end boulders away from the dikes and the Army Corps of Engineers would come along with big barges and a crane to reposition and build the dikes back up. It was a continuing process of man trying to control the river. The men I was eating lunch with were responsible for surveying and determining the work that needed to be done to keep the dikes in shape. They also told me that occasionally winds coming up river were strong enough to create 8 to 10 foot waves.

These guys really seemed to be enjoying their job. At night they would either pitch a tent or, if they were close to a town, go to a motel. They had all kinds of river stories. We had a fine conversation and lots of fun. As I left, I paddled back upstream a little so that I might get their picture as I went by.

On Tuesday, October 14th, I arrived outside of the town of Hermann. It was by far the prettiest town I had seen on my trip. The folks here were of German heritage. The architecture of the houses and commercial buildings reflected that of the old country. Many of the streets were cobblestone and well-preserved. I believe the town had at least five to ten wineries.

In the summer the population surged from around 1500 to 5000 as the tourists flocked in. Bed and breakfast establishments were evident all over town and there were some old hotels too. As pretty as the town was, the people were just as friendly. That isn't true in a lot of tourist havens. Sometimes the locals get sick of seeing strangers invading, but not the folks here.

Several boats were tied up outside of this old bait shop. I guided the canoe in and secured it to the dock. I peeked through the door glass and could see an old guy bent over a chopping block. When I knocked on the door, there was a friendly response, "Come on in!" I introduced myself and he said his name was Dallas.

He was busy cutting carp into skinny little pieces. Along with the bait shop, he did some commercial fishing, and these fish pieces would be packaged and sold to local stores. The man was really friendly. I told him what I was doing and said that I was looking for a place to put my bedroll for the night. He said the temperature was supposed to be in the 30's. If I didn't mind, he said he could find a place on the basement floor for me to lay my tarp down for the night. The basement was where he kept his live bait. A water heater there took off the chill. I told him that would be great. He said he would leave the door unlocked and I could come and go as I wanted to. Also he invited me up to a local restaurant for coffee the next morning. Said he was usually up there by 6 a.m.

It never failed to amaze me how people along this river would go out of their way to help a stranger. Even the fact that he would leave his bait storage area unlocked for me to stay exemplified his willingness to trust me. Maybe I just had an honest-looking face.

I had this strong urge for some of Grandma's homemade apple crisp dessert, so I went up to the store and bought some apples and other ingredients. I wasn't sure how I was going to make it, but a strong appetite can do wonders for one's inventiveness.

I took my kettle and put about three big handfuls of sand in the bottom. I thought that if the kettle was on the flame for a long time, the sand might insulate it enough to keep it from being burned. I cut the apples into slices and put them in another pot. Over the top I sprinkled brown sugar, oatmeal and cinnamon. I put the smaller pot into the one with the sand and put a lid on. After pumping up the stove fuel bottle, I lit it and turned the flame down to simmer. I would let it cook for 1-1/2 hours, while I explored town.

I took my time looking at all the beautifully restored homes in Hermann. The city was lighted with old-time lamplights and everything was so clean and neat. I visited with a couple of the residents, then made some phone calls home. Before heading back I also picked up quite a few groceries. I completely forgot about the apple crisp. When I got back, the gas had shut itself off because of low pressure, but the kettle was still hot. The apple crisp was burned just a tiny bit on the top, however it tasted great and I ate the whole thing.

With my bedroll all set up in the shed I went right to sleep. The railroad tracks were not far away and I did wake to a passing freight train, but was soon back to sleep.

Shortly after 6 a.m. I met the bait shop owner in the coffee shop. I ordered a hearty breakfast of ham, eggs, an English muffin and coffee. My friend introduced me to another guy who was interested in my trip. It turns out he was a reporter for the town newspaper.

About 7:30 I started to excuse myself, to leave for the river. I said, "I'll sure remember Hermann. I'm very impressed with your town."

"We're very proud of our town too. I'd like to get some pictures of you down by the river if you don't mind."

There was a three-foot layer of fog on the river. I would wait until that cleared before I left. I didn't want a barge that I couldn't see or hear running me down. Because of the fog I had a few minutes to kill, so I began packing food while I chewed the fat with the reporter and Dallas. When the fog lifted enough, the reporter took a couple of pictures and I was on my way. Not far outside of Hermann I met an Amtrak train going in the opposite direction. It had slowed to pass through the town. I waved to the engineer and he waved back, then hit his horn three times. I could see the passengers in the train dining car picture windows eating their breakfast. They waved too. There was still a light layer of fog on the river and I'll bet the lone canoer on the river made an impressionable picture for them to see.

I had less than 100 miles to go before the Missouri joined the Mississippi. It was Tuesday, and Dad wouldn't be here until Saturday to pick me up. There was no reason to rush. Washington was the next town. That was about 40 miles from Hermann and would be far enough for today. The river current had slowed considerably and there were numerous large islands in the river now.

I approached Washington around 4 p.m. There was a breaker wall extending into the river that I had to paddle around, but the public boat ramp and dock were on a bend, so the current allowed me to glide right up to the dock.

I stuffed my dirty laundry into my knapsack, then buttoned up the canoe. The way the canoe was tied, the dock pretty well hid it from view. A person would actually have to be out on the dock to see it.

A couple sets of railroad tracks bordered the park and on the other side was town. I stopped at a car dealership for directions to the laundromat. It turned out to be only a half-mile away.

After getting my laundry started, I sat down for a few minutes and watched the news on TV. It was the first time I had watched TV since leaving Michigan. A couple of elderly ladies were also sitting there waiting for their laundry and I had a brief conversation with them. A real pretty girl came in with her wash while we were talking.

I was quite dirty. I had brought my shaving kit and a towel along to clean myself up in the laundromat restroom. I locked the door behind me and stripped down for a sponge bath. Then I washed my hair, shaved, brushed my teeth and put on some clean clothes.

When I came out the pretty girl was still there. She was a tall blonde and I couldn't help noticing her nice figure as she was bending over by the machines. Besides her good looks, she had arrived in a pickup truck. That certainly was a plus.

There must have been something wrong with her truck engine though, for she had left the hood up. Her boyfriend soon arrived on the scene and she went out to meet him. He's dressed like a mechanic. Now I can hear him yelling at her about the truck. I don't know what it's all about but the yelling gets worse and he's really cussing her out. It's time for me to rescue this pretty young thing. I go out to offer my assistance.

"What's the problem here? Do you need some help with a jump start or something?" The boyfriend cooled right down and that brought a relieved smile from the girl.

"No thank you," he said. "It's a bigger problem than that."

I went back inside and visited some more with the older ladies. The girl and her boyfriend soon left in his truck.

Further along on the river there was a combination bar-restaurant right near the shoreline. It was about dusk and my stomach was crying for food. With my clean laundry packed away, I walked down for something to eat.

While they were preparing my wet burrito, I enjoyed a beer. The burrito really tasted good. I guzzled down another beer with my food and relaxed with one more after dinner. I was in a mellow mood. My trip was almost over and from here on there was no reason to rush. I could just take my time, enjoy myself and spend a couple of days seeing the sights of St. Louis when I got there. It was about 9:30; not very late, but I was ready for bed anyway. I brushed my teeth, spread out my bedroll and placed the bags with the clean laundry down for my pillow. I laid my clothes on the dock and crawled into the sleeping bag with only my underwear on. There was a nice light breeze. Soon I was fast asleep.

I was used to hearing trains go by at night. They would wake me, but not for long. About 1:30 or 2 a.m. this freight train went through, and after it passed I was just dozing off again, when up on the hill I heard someone stumbling around in the grass, then start cussing. Moments later it was quiet again, until I heard the heavy boots coming down my dock in an uneven pace. There was enough light from the moon to see that someone was carrying a bag over their shoulder and, with the assistance of the dock handrail, staggering in my direction. I started to sit up in my sleeping bag. I'm trying to make out who this person is that's coming so close. "What's going on here?" I said.

The response was more of a gruff mumbling. I'm not sure whether he tripped or just intentionally dropped down, but he landed right on top of me with both his bags. And in my face was this head with bushy hair, a goatee and breath that reeked of alcohol. There was a large split in his chin and blood was running down through his goatee and on to his neck.

"Get off," I said. In a daze, I tried to sit up more, but his full weight was spread across my stomach and he didn't offer to move.

In slurry detail I started hearing his story. He and his buddy, or someone he had just met on the train, were sharing a fifth of tequila in a boxcar on the freight train. Something was said that pissed the other guy off. The friendship ended and a fight broke out. Apparently the other guy was bigger and this dude decided to get his bags and exit the boxcar.

Even though the trains slow some going through town, they still are moving at a pretty good clip. I could see why this guy was cut up as there is nothing but asphalt and concrete near the tracks.

I was nervous and I didn't know exactly how to handle this drunk. The first thing I needed to do was to get him off of me.

"You've got a pretty bad cut on your chin. I've got a first-aid kit. Why don't we try to fix that up."

While I was offering the first aid, I tried to slide from the sleeping bag and out from underneath him. I was part way out when he grabbed my arm. "Just get back in your bag."

"You look like you're hurting. I think we should fix up that cut."

"Naw, you just get back in your sleeping bag."

As I slid my legs back in the sleeping bag, my mind raced at computer speed for a solution to this predicament. I had never dealt with a belligerent drunk before, but I had the distinct impression that he could be a time bomb waiting to go off. The gallant thing to do would be to wrestle him off and kick his ass in the water. I wasn't sure how successful I would be doing this. The guy was as big or bigger than I was, and being partially trapped in the sleeping bag with his full weight on me, my moves would be hindered from the start. Also I had nothing on but my underwear. I wondered, too, that if all of a sudden this guy perceived me as a threat, I might also be confronted with a knife.

Even though I felt horribly vulnerable, for now, my choices seemed limited. I decided that I would play it cool and not antagonize this dude. I tried to get a conversation going.

"Where ya from?"

"I just got out of prison down in Texas. I'm on my way to Alaska. That's where I'm from. My name is Tobias. That's my Indian name."

He then noticed my canoe. "Hey, someone left a canoe down here."

"That's my canoe. I'm canoeing down the river to St. Louis."

He then kinda fell back down and buried his elbow in my chest.

"Hey man, knock it off; that hurts."

Then he says, "You're not gay, are ya?"

"No, I'm not gay."

"I had enough of those gay guys in prison."

This fella is right in my face with his boozy breath. I try to keep him talking, but already I can envision that sooner or later I'm going to have to take action. I'm not sure how that's going to work out. He's fully clothed with cowboy boots on and is pretty well numbed to reality by the alcohol. Jumping off a train didn't phase him, a fight on this dock would be child's play.

On the other hand, here I am in my underwear at 2 a.m. on the end of a dock. I'll try to keep him talking. Maybe he'll settle down. Before I could say anything more he said, "You know, I like you. I'm gonna go steal us a couple of fishing poles and we'll sit on the end of this dock and fish all night. Ya like to fish, don't ya?"

"Yes, but it's a little late, don't you think?"

He pushed his bedroll and clothes bag down on my stomach. "I'm gonna leave my stuff right here. Don't you even think about stealing it. If you do I'll remember your face and come looking for ya."

"Don't worry," I said. "It'll be here when you get back."

I watched him walk off the dock and up the hill towards the tracks. I was out of my sleeping bag collecting my clothes and I could see he had stopped and was watching me. I just stood quiet until he started out again and disappeared over the hill.

With my pants on I decided that the first priority was to get my transportation out of here ready. I unbuttoned the canoe canvas, got my paddle out and snapped the two halves together. I untied the canoe, climbed in, and started scooping my sleeping bag, mattress, shoes and laundry bag off the dock. Everything was just piled on the canoe in a disorderly fashion. At any moment I expected to see him racing back down the hill and out on the dock.

I dug the paddle in and started up river. There was another dock a quarter-mile in that direction. My action spooked a bunch of ducks and they all flew off quacking; probably pissed that I had ruined their night's rest.

I hoped that I could get out of sight before he returned and saw the direction I was headed. For a few moments I just glided and listened; nothing.

My pace upstream was relentless. The quicker I put some distance between myself and this dock the better off I'd be.

I found the dock I remembered and pulled up to where the refueling shed was. After securing the canoe, I threw my shoes up on the dock and, with the shotgun, climbed out and finished dressing. Even though I had no intention of shooting the guy, if old Tobias showed up down here I think even in his state of mind he might back off if I threatened him with the gun. I'm sure a shot over his head would do it, too. Anyway, it was loaded and at least now I felt confident that I had more control of the situation.

I followed the gangplank past the few boats that were tied up, and low and behold, at the end of the dock was a pay phone; what luck. I inserted my quarter and called 911.

When the dispatcher answered I said, "Ma'am, this is not an emergency, but down at the public dock I was sleeping, minding my own business, when this hobo filled with tequila jumped off the train and started harassing me."

I described my location. Then she said, "I'll have a patrol car come right down. What does this guy look like?"

"Well he's tall, probably over six feet, has got long hair and a goatee."

All of a sudden, I realized that my description of him was like a description of myself.

"Say, I need to tell you that I look a lot like the guy I'm describing." In the background I could hear her radio the patrol car. "The man calling says he looks a lot like the hobo."

"Where is the hobo now?"

"He went off to steal some fishing poles."

"OK, a car will be right down, stay on the phone."

In the distance I could hear the sirens. Soon there were the flashing lights of two cruisers at the public dock.

"Sir, the officers have got the offender's property, but he's not there. Stay at the phone and they'll be right down to talk with you."

I didn't wonder that they didn't see old Tobias. With the sirens and flashing lights, he wasn't about to hang around.

The officers arrived and I explained the situation to them. After they took their report, they said they'd check out the area again;

maybe they'd see the guy. They asked where I would be staying. I pointed to the rock barrier out in the river.

"Well, I was thinking of staying out there."

About five minutes after they left, the officers were right back down at the public dock with all their lights flashing. Old Tobias was not dumb enough to show himself. He was probably watching from a clump of bushes. He was also probably really pissed that they had confiscated his belongings.

That was the last time the police were around that night. I paddled out to the rock barrier, but there was no way I could sleep on those big boulders. I went back and put my bedroll inside the fueling shed at the end of the dock where I had called the police. I had to fix up some kind of booby trap to keep Tobias from showing up unannounced again. I knew that he would be anxious to get his hands on me.

Out of my backpack I got a spool of 40-pound fishing line. I weaved it back and forth across the gangplank at various heights. I would tie it off at regular intervals so that anyone trying to cut their way through would have to make several cuts. It took a half-hour and probably 200 feet of fishing line, but I had assembled a web that any self-respecting spider would be proud of. I thought that even I would have a rough time getting through it in the daytime, let alone at night.

It was about 3 a.m. when I laid down to rest. The shotgun was right beside me and I did get to sleep. When a wave came in to rock a boat, creating a creaking noise, I woke right up. I really didn't expect to see the hobo, but I wanted to be on the safe side. Once I woke up and imagined he was standing in the doorway. I was almost at the end of my trip and self-preservation was paramount in my mind.

St. Louis

October 16th to October 19th

I was on my way before sunrise. A two-foot bank of fog covered the water and the canoe, but I was above it. Traveling through the fog was neat, rather mystical. (This sunrise pictured on back cover.)

There was much less river current now. Even though I didn't have many miles to travel, it was slow going. The St. Louis City limits was 25 miles away, but already I was passing through its suburb communities, Chesterfield, Maryland Heights, St. Charles. I took a break around lunchtime and walked to a party store for a pop tart and sandwich.

I knew that I could easily make the Mississippi River by nightfall. I thought it would be much more fitting, however, to cross into it in the morning. For that reason I started looking for a place to camp early, around 6 p.m.

At a gravel company, three tugboats were tied up. It didn't look like anyone was around so I decided to sleep on one of them. I picked the one with the new paint job; that should be the cleanest.

The deck was four feet off the water, so it was a little extra work pulling my gear up from the canoe. I lit the stove to boil my supper water, then inflated my mattresss, spread the bedroll and turned on the radio. The weather was perfect and my meal was satisfying. All in all I was in a great mood, even singing and whistling along with the radio tunes. Around 10 p.m. I fell asleep. Three hours later I woke up and turned the radio off.

Fog was on the river in the morning, but not enough to delay my departure.

I didn't eat any breakfast because I had a plan to cook my final batch of french toast right in front of the St. Louis Arch. It took two hours to reach the Mississippi, and then I wasn't sure I was really on it. The channel was on the east side; that's where the boat traffic was. The west side was like a big flood plain. According to the map, there was a large rock dam somewhere ahead. I didn't know whether I would have to pull my canoe over it or if there was a place to go around.

Up ahead there were huge columns of cement left over from an old bridge. The bridge was long gone, but someone had built a very picturesque house on one of the columns. It was a neat little house with a copper roof. Later I would learn that the people who had lived there finally donated it to the city as an historical sight. I took a picture as I went by.

Now I could see the line of boulders ahead. It reminded me of the diversion dams on the Yellowstone. I could see a washed out area in the center, however the flow was really swift there and it might be shallow. This close to my goal, I didn't want to smash up the canoe. It was better to play it safe and plan a different way around. As I got closer I could see the rocks extended for 100 feet or so. I didn't relish unloading all my gear to make numerous trips to get on the other side.

There was a lagoon on the west side near the dam and I saw a boat with two men pull into it. I brought my canoe up to the edge of the rock dam, tied it off and climbed up on a pile of logs to look down into the lagoon on the other side. The two men sat in the boat reading a newspaper.

"Good morning," I yelled down. "I'm Scott Galloway canoeing down from Billings, Montana."

I climbed down the other side and chatted with them for awhile. They worked for the Army Corps of Engineers and charted water levels along the river. They gave me more information on the house built on the bridge pylon up river, but they couldn't offer any easy route around this dam. I said good-bye and they wished me luck.

By this time my stomach was really growling. I needed to get beyond this dam so I could get some breakfast. There were several medium-sized pieces of driftwood nearby, so I rigged a trail of logs laid crosswise to pull the canoe over the rocks. I'd move the canoe forward on a bunch, then bring some more around front and move it a little more. The process was not real fast, but at least I didn't have to unload everything, carry it all, then reload.

Once on the other side of the dam, I had about ten miles to go before I reached the St. Louis Arch. I could already see the arch, though. Its stainless steel coating glistened in the morning sunlight.

Everything was really coming together nicely. I was ecstatic over the fact that I had made it all this way and my goal was actually in sight. It was also good that I had delayed the last of this journey until morning. It was so beautiful just to see it all in the early morning sunshine.

Now there were large ports on the river. I met numerous barges loaded with coal, grain, oil, and chemicals. They were going real slow and their wake caused me no problem. Most of the tugboat captains waved.

It was 11 a.m. when I pulled up to the cobblestone levee in front of the arch. I positioned two big driftwood logs to skid the canoe out on. I stood there for several minutes just looking at the arch and trying to soak up all the grandeur of the moment. Was I really glad this trip had ended? The answer to that question was an easy no. If I didn't have a job waiting and a girl friend back in Michigan, I would be just as happy to continue right on down the Mississippi. In fact, there was just a twinge of disappointment in not being able to do that. The river seemed to be calling me. "Come on, Scott, there are lots of adventures waiting for you if you just follow me."

The reality of my hunger shoved the dream world aside for the moment. I had lots of eggs and bread left, so it was time for one more big french toast breakfast. Out with the stove and skillet; what better place could I have for my last breakfast, than right here in front of the arch. Probably there was some city ordinance against this but I wasn't going to wait to find out.

Tourists were starting to make their way around the arch grounds, and several noticed the lone canoe and river rat cooking his breakfast on the levee. Some thought I was just preparing to start my trip; others were just curious as to what I was up to. In between mouthfuls of french toast I answered their questions and tried to be cordial.

Now I wanted to see the sights of St. Louis. I paddled down to the large casino boat and introduced myself to the security guard.

"Sure, I'll watch your canoe. Your stuff will be safe, go have a good time," he said.

With some clean clothes on, I headed for the arch. It wasn't long before I was at the top enjoying a most spectacular view of St. Louis. I could even see my canoe, and it looked like a toy. Next I bought tickets to three different movies they were showing in the theater below. One was taken during all of the arch construction. It was quite interesting.

There also was a very nice western museum underneath the arch. I toured that, then spent the rest of the afternoon just lying on the grass outside, reading the newspaper, my Louis and Clark book and taking naps. How nice it was to wake up and just look up in the sky at that big old arch in the blue October sky. To sum it all up, I was just savoring my success.

My plan was to put my bedroll up on the arch grounds some-where. There were cops all over the place, however, and I could see that wasn't going to be acceptable. Instead I spread my bedroll right on the large granite cobblestones that formed the levee. They were still nice and warm from the sun. I fixed up a pot of hot chocolate and just sat there enjoying the waterfront scenery when this man with a hunting jacket and boots stopped. He was interested in my trip and told me about his adventure on the Appalachian Trail. I asked him if a cup of hot chocolate would taste good. "Sure," he said.

Even though our trips were completely different, there was a natural appreciation and understanding of what the other had accomplished. We talked for well over an hour.

"Hey, I'm hungry," he said. "Why don't we go over to the casino boat and enjoy their all-you-can-eat buffet? I'll treat, just to make up for all the folks who bought me dinner on the trail."

I put my bedroll back in the canoe and buttoned it up. There was a ramp going out to the tour boat dock. I tied the canoe to that.

We had a great meal and I really stuffed myself. I found out that my friend worked with troubled kids as a counselor. He would take groups of them on camping trips. We talked for two more hours after dinner, then exchanged telephone numbers and said good-bye. It had been an absolutely great day in St. Louis. I looked forward to crawling into my sleeping bag on the levee and just drifting off to sleep with the river noises in the background. That was not to be.

The area on the levee where I had left my canoe was busy during the daytime, but at night there was no commercial activity. The big casino boat was always busy, but it was tied to the shore 200 yards up river. It was Friday night, and when I returned from the casino boat there were a large number of cars parked near the canoe and a big party taking place on the levee. Apparently this was the big late night hangout for St. Louis's young black people. I debated whether or not I should get my bedroll back out. There were a lot of eyes on me and some unpleasant racial remarks came in my direction. This was their territory and in no uncertain terms they let me know I was not welcome.

I unbuttoned the canoe, got my paddle out and climbed in. I would spend the rest of the night away from here, probably on the other side of the river. The "white boy" jeers got a little louder as I paddled off. They were elated at their success in driving me away.

It was a miserable night on the other side of the river. There wasn't a good place for my bedroll, plus the river boats came by very close, and kept me awake. I wasn't even sure how safe this side was. I kept the shotgun loaded and within arm's reach.

In the morning I crossed the river, tied the canoe in my previous spot and went down to the casino boat for the buffet breakfast. In the breakfast line I met some guys that were planning to tour the Budweiser Brewery and they invited me along. The security guard willingly agreed to watch my canoe again, so I was off for the tour. That turned out to be a really neat trip, with the opportunity to sample several different kinds of beer. The guys I was with were a lot of fun too.

The rest of Saturday was spent the same as Friday, lying in the grass under the arch reading. Dad was supposed to arrive a little after 6 p.m., so around 5:30 I positioned myself on a bench beside the waterfront road.

At 10 minutes before six I heard a familiar voice yell, "What you up to, kid?" There in the opposite lane was Dad's old cruddy-looking '77 Ford pickup. But it was an absolutely beautiful sight. I was ecstatic; just totally happy to see his smiling face and that familiar old truck. He drove on down the road until he could find a place to turn around, then came back and parked beside some other cars on the levee. There was a big hug, and it was really hard to know where to begin. There was so much he wanted to know and so much that I needed to tell him.

Before the sun went down he wanted some pictures of me in the canoe in front of the arch. To actually get the arch in the background of any picture, he would have had to be in the middle of the river, so he settled for pictures along the shoreline.

We sat and talked for awhile, then I suggested the casino boat buffet. Dad thought that it would be better to put the canoe up near the truck and secure it to the side of the truck with some rope. Except for the gun, we left the gear in the canoe and just buttoned it up. The gun went behind the seat in the truck.

There was a cap on the back of the truck and Dad had a couple of cots back there. The plan was to sleep in the back tonight, then get some more pictures in the early morning before we left.

Although we had to stand in line for 45 minutes, we both thought that it was a great meal. When we left the dining room and walked through the lower levels there was someone in front of every slot machine, and each gaming table was crowded. It was Saturday night and the place was packed.

It was around 9:30 and Dad decided to start taping part of my story for this book. He got his recorder out of the truck, we checked the canoe and then started across the levee to where the two tour boats were docked. On the way a couple of young blacks were walking towards us and one asked Dad if he had a light. Dad didn't, but I had a lighter and lit the guy's cigarette. He said thanks and asked how we were doing.

We found a nice table on the dock and Dad hooked up his recorder to the mike. The only activity at this time of night was the people cleaning up the tour boats from the day's run. The truck was less than two hundred feet away. It was the only vehicle down on this part of the levee.

The evening was absolutely beautiful. The world's biggest casino river boat was going up and down the river all lit up nice and pretty and there were the horns from that and the tugboats. It was cool out, but we both had light jackets on and there was only a little breeze. Even the smell of the river was pleasant.

Before we started recording, Dad turned the tape recorder on to play. It was Ted Nugent's song about Fred Bear. As the distinctive guitar sounds rolled out, the tour boat cleaning people looked out with a "what the hell's going on out here?" look on their faces. I thought they might try to run us off, but they just smiled and continued their work. The song is one of Dad's favorites and as out of place as it might seem, the catchy ballad fit right in with the night's atmosphere.

We started out with Dad asking me a few leading questions about the trip. Then he just sat back and took notes as my story rolled out. We had only recorded for a half-hour when I noticed him staring over towards the truck. Reaching up, he stopped the recorder and said, "Scott, I don't see the canoe." I looked around and couldn't see it either. Maybe there just wasn't enough light to see it. I walked down the ramp and across the levee towards the truck. I could see it was gone. Dad hurriedly bagged up his recording stuff and followed me. Halfway to the truck he caught one foot on a stone and went down hard on his knee and hands. When he got up I could see the palm of one hand was really bleeding.

The canoe was nowhere in sight. One of the ropes tying it to the truck had been cut, the other untied. Neither one of us could understand how anyone could have possibly taken it in just that short period of time while we sat up on the dock. The canoe was in our view all of the time and only a couple hundred feet away. We couldn't believe it had happened and it was not the way we wanted to end this fine evening. It gave both of us a really sick feeling.

Everyone that drove down to the levee had to pass by a guarded ticket entrance, so I asked Dad if he would check with them while I looked around more and called the police.

I called the police station twice. Twenty minutes after the first call no one showed up so I called again. A lost canoe at 11 p.m. at night probably wasn't a high priority in East St. Louis. It was to me though.

The officer that arrived seemed sympathetic to my situation. He took a report, then asked me to climb in and we drove back and forth along the levee looking for the canoe in the water. He kept asking if I didn't think the canoe just drifted away. I said that either someone had driven off with it, or paddled it away on the river. He suggested that it might have just been set adrift in the water. I told him that the only people I saw on the levee near the truck were the two black guys. The officer was black too and he took a little offense at my quick assumption that these guys were the culprits. He said, "Black people don't like water that well; don't just assume they took your canoe out into the river."

I could understand what he was trying to tell me, but I also knew there had been no one else around. We drove back up on the road and I saw Dad coming back. I got his attention and he came over to the patrol car. He said that the intersection security people had seen no one leave with a canoe. The security people at the casino had seen nothing either, but they insisted that Dad let one of their people look after his hand. They took him down to the aid room, cleaned up and bandaged his hand and also his knee which had a large scrape.

The officer told us that if we found the canoe to please let him know. He left his card.

There were about eight or ten barges tied up a half-mile down river. If, in fact, someone had just pushed the canoe in the water for the hell of it, the current would take it in that direction. Maybe it would stop next to the barges. I could see that Dad thought the canoe was a goner, but he seemed willing to keep looking. It was hard for either of us to accept the fact that, after all I had been through, my $1500 canoe, and all my gear were gone. Stolen from right under our noses. It would be one hell of a somber ride back to Michigan.

We walked down towards the barges. It was pretty isolated and mostly unlit at this time of night. The McDonalds floating restaurant was on the left but it had been closed for a couple of hours. There was one lone car driving around on the levee. It would stop for awhile in one place, then later you would see it parked somewhere else. I don't think either one of us was at ease in this environment.

As we moved closer I could see men working on the barges. A tugboat was positioned on the up river side and its floodlight covered the work area with light. We had to climb down an embankment to reach the closest point to the barges. Probably they were out 10 feet or so from the shoreline.

The tugboat's diesel engines were making a fair amount of noise, so I had to yell to get the nearest workman's attention. He came over on the closest barge.

"Hey, someone stole my canoe a few hours ago. I wondered if you could tell the captain to keep an eye out for it in the river."

He shouted back, "We just found a white canoe against the barges a little while ago. It was full of water. We fished it out and put it on the deck of the tug."

About the time he answered me I could hear the captain's voice coming over the guy's radio. "What the hell's going on down there?"

"We just found the guy who lost the canoe we picked up."

"I don't give a shit about that canoe. We have to get these barges ready to go. Now get your asses busy or I'll personally throw that god-damned canoe back in the river."

The workman said, "I've got to get back to work. We'll think of something."

Dad and I were overjoyed with the fact that the canoe had shown up. Of course we were a long ways from having our hands on it or knowing what kind of shape it was in, but at least we knew where it was.

We thought it would be best if one of us stayed here to keep an eye on things. Dad volunteered to walk back and see if he could find a rowboat or some other way of getting out to the tug. I sat there trying to figure a way to get from shore to the deck of that nearest barge. It would be worth the risk of the captain's wrath if I could get to the canoe. If I did that, I could figure some way to get it back onshore.

I walked down the shoreline and located a pretty long piece of driftwood. I leaned it against the side of the barge and skinned up it until I could reach the steel bar that held the two strands of barbed wire that went around the top of the deck. The bar was rusty, it started to break off. I grabbed below the break with the other hand and pulled myself up high enough to get a foot on top. The rest was easy.

I made my way across the barges towards the tug. The captain eventually noticed me in his floodlight. Over the loudspeaker he said to his workers, "Tell that guy he's not allowed on my boat."

It was too late. I was already over there and climbing up on the tug. Come hell or high water I was planning to get the canoe. Maybe both the canoe and I would end up thrown in the water.

The captain came down out of the wheelhouse, "I don't know how you're going to get your canoe back, we're too busy now ... how'd it get away from ya anyway?"

I spit my story out as quickly as I could, "Captain I just canoed here from Billings, Montana and some kids untied the canoe from our truck and threw it in the water. I just want to get it off your boat and go home."

The captain now seemed to have a more congenial outlook on my situation. It was obvious that it would be quite a drop to the water to get the canoe off the tug, so he hollered to one of his workers to come aboard, then backed his tug up to the dock a hundred yards up river. I had him shine his floodlight up onshore as we moved towards the dock, and the beam picked up Dad walking towards the barges. I hollered as loud as I could over the diesel engines and the captain moved the light back and forth to get his attention. Dad got the message. He started towards the same dock. By the time he found his way through the ship maintenance yard to the dock, we had already unloaded the canoe and the tug was on its way back to the barges.

Everything inside the canoe was soaked. We took all my gear out, drained the canoe again, then piled my stuff back in. There didn't seem to be any damage to the canoe other than several extra scratches from where it banged up against the barges.

We carried the canoe to a lower dock and put it into the water. I would paddle it back to where the truck was. Dad said that there was a carload of young blacks driving around watching him walk back and forth on the levee. He thought that perhaps they were responsible. They had gone by and he could see they were laughing about something.

Back at the tour boat docks I tied the canoe up and Dad drove the truck down close. I left him there watching things while I went up to call the officer and tell him we had found the canoe.

When I left to call the police officer our truck was the only vehicle on that part of the levee. When I returned there were 8 to 10 cars all within 50 feet of the truck and the young St. Louis blacks had their party going full blast again, just as they had the previous night. A large ghetto blaster was cranking out music, girls were dancing on the cobblestones and a few guys were rolling dice in a crap game. Dad looked a tad bit uncomfortable. The kids were all nicely dressed and just seemed to be having a good time, but we thought that we wouldn't be getting much sleep in the back of the truck here tonight. We decided to move closer to the main casino, which was docked a couple hundred yards up river. As I started pushing off from the shore a girl came down close to the water and said, "Can I have a ride in your canoe?"

"Sorry, not tonight," I said.

Dad moved the truck down and waited while I paddled down to the casino boat. There were a lot of cars going and coming from that parking lot. It was obvious if we stayed there it was going to be noisy all night. Dad said, "Scott, let's go get a motel room."

With the canoe tied in the truck we drove across the Mississippi and tried to find a motel room. Two motels were full, but on our last try we lucked out and got a room. It was 3 a.m. and we were exhausted. I took my first hot shower in weeks and Dad just went to bed. The motel room wasn't great, but it was better than the cots would have been in the back of the truck on the levee. What a night it had been, but at least we had the canoe and a warm room to sleep in.

Top: Chamberlain, S.D. Photo courtesy of Oacoma Register.

Bottom: Shane Haire – helped patch the canoe – Sioux City.

Top: Sand dredge.

Bottom: Leo and his daughter fishing – Boonville, Mo.

Top: Surveyors I ate lunch with – after Jefferson City, Mo.

Bottom: River boat – One of many things named after Lewis and Clark.

Top: At the motel ready to head home.

Bottom: Journey's end. Scott and the Bell Magic at the Arch of St. Louis.

Going Home

By 8:30 the next morning we were up and ready to head towards Michigan. Dad had backed the truck into a parking place next to the office. The motel clerk had promised to keep an eye on it while we were sleeping.

A continental breakfast came with the room so we had a roll and coffee before leaving. Dad decided that it wasn't worth it to drive all the way back to the arch for more pictures, but we did walk to the edge of the parking lot for one last look. At least the tip of the arch was visible. With a good night's sleep and the canoe securely tied in the back of the truck, we were in fine spirits.

Before long we were on the expressway heading towards Indianapolis. There we would join a different freeway that would take us all the way to Michigan.

The old '77 Ford truck was running smooth as could be. Dad said that it had only burned a half quart of oil to St. Louis. With a manual stick shift on the steering column, this old girl had no power steering and was well rusted, but to look at Dad over there, you would have thought he was driving a brand new Cadillac.

The sun finally found its way through the clouds and it was warm enough to have the truck windows down. We both were tired of talking so other than the truck noise it was quiet. So many unexpected things had happened last night, it just seemed that there hadn't been enough time to put my trip in perspective. There needed to be some profound spiritual-type finale to all of this.

Even though I had just spent almost two months of my life paddling down the Yellowstone and Missouri Rivers, it seemed like it had all taken place ages ago. I was right back in the middle of civilization and sharing my day with everyone else on this road. The end seemed so anticlimactic.

I did have two big things to be thankful for. I was alive and the Bell Magic was safe in the back of the truck. Probably the rest of it was all small potatoes.

My experience with those young black people in St. Louis wasn't a pleasant one, but then I remembered what had happened to Eddy Harris, the black man, in the book **MISSISSIPPI SOLO**. Two boozed up southern white hunters had invaded his camp and threatened him with their guns. He escaped into the underbrush and scared them off by firing over their heads with his pistol. My confrontation wasn't nearly as dangerous.

As I retraced the trip in my mind, I remembered the times when I thought my life was in jeopardy. Those events didn't seem that harrowing now, but still a lot had happened to me. For 2400 miles I had watched these rivers. I did feel that I had been more than just a spectator. When their moods changed I was there. You can look at a scenic river picture and say that's nice, but I think I really felt like I had been part of that picture; at least for a moment in time.

I wondered how many people now knew about my trip. A lone canoeist on these rivers was unique enough to spark interest. Those that saw me probably told friends, relatives, and coworkers that they had seen someone canoeing to St. Louis. How many ears would hear about that? How far would the story travel? And yet, whenever I asked someone for directions, no one seemed to know much about what went on down river. If I was living on the banks of the Missouri, the not-knowing would eat me alive. How could one live there and not have knowledge of the river, at least as far as the next major city or next state?

The old Ford hummed along. I laid my head back and closed my eyes. I thought about all the people along the river that had gone out of their way to help me; there were so many that wanted me to succeed. It was like this was their trip too, and really it was. What made me chuckle was that everyone that wanted to hear my tale had a story of their own to tell. It was like my adventure gave importance to theirs.

I was getting sleepy. Dad looked awake, so I would doze off for awhile. Then out of the blue I remembered at the start of my trip, only a few miles down the Yellowstone, I had pulled out and asked for God's help to keep me safe, and the river spirits to look after me too. I felt a little embarrassed. Not until now was I getting around to say, "Thanks."

Left: The author – Gordon Galloway.

Right: The River Rat – Scott Galloway and the 1977 Ford at home.

Equipment Critique

THUMBS UP!

CANOE – After being married to the Bell Magic for 2400 miles, I am still enthusiastic over its outstanding performance.

CANOE COVER – Without this cover I would have had to add two weeks to the trip because of rough weather. Thanks to Cooks Custom Sewing.

DOUBLE BLADED PADDLE – With a double blade you never waste a stroke. And, when you're turning out 12,000 strokes a day, that's important. I can't imagine going back to a single blade.

CRAZY CREEK CANOE CHAIR – I would have had one sore back if I didn't have it. Imagine sitting down 8-12 hours a day for 52 days with nothing to lean on.

THERMOREST MATTRESS – Nothing better than sleeping on air after a hard day.

GAS COOKSTOVE – Reliable in all kinds of weather when hot food and drink are real morale boosters. Uses just regular gasoline, which is always available.

SPONGE – This little item came in real handy for keeping the canoe dry and clean, not to mention wiping off muddy feet.

HAT CLIP – Without this my hat would have ended up in the drink many times.

RADIO (headphones) – When the scenery was unchanging for hundreds of miles, I was happy I had brought it along.

LEATHERMAN PLIERS – Continually came in handy.

PADDLE GLOVES – Although my hands were dry and cracked in some places, the fingerless leather gloves took most of the abuse.

CAST-IRON SKILLET (10 inch) – This was fairly heavy but well worth having along. Once you learn to cook on one, there's nothing that comes close.

THERMOS – Coffee, mixed with a little hot chocolate, powdered milk and condensed sweetened milk, makes for a great mid-morning break.

FLASHLIGHT – The mini mag light was small and light enough to fit in my belt holster.

EMERGENCY BLANKET (reflective) – Foil-lined on the inside. It radiated heat back at me and kept the dew off in the morning.

THUMBS DOWN!

RIVER SANDALS – Every time I put them on I had a bad experience. They either rubbed my feet raw or got stuck in the mud.

SAILING RIG (6 lbs.) – I initially spent 10 hours fabricating it, then hauled it the whole way only to use successfully for 10 miles.

LANTERN (3 lbs.) – The lantern came in handy once, for catfishing on the Yellowstone. Other times it just leaked fuel and, when lit, drew the mosquitoes right to me.

TENT (12 lbs.) – It was a large GeoDome 4 man. I think I was glad to see it sink to the bottom of the river. I had a much more enjoyable time sleeping on boat ramps, docks and on the beach. When it rained I always managed to find shelter.

CHANGES FOR MY NEXT TRIP

WATER PURIFIER – They say that coffee filters wrapped around the intake and secured by a rubber band do an excellent job of prefiltering water before it reaches the purifier. Probably this would lengthen its life considerably.

GUN – I didn't use the 22 mag that much. The shotgun alone would have been fine and saved weight.

The Fifty Things To Do In Life Philosophy

by Scott Galloway

There is one last thing I would like to say before we end this book. It's about living your life to the fullest. While on this canoe trip, so many people told me, "I wish I would have done something like this when I was younger." You can't imagine what a warm, satisfying feeling I get, knowing that I picked out one of my dreams and hell or high water saw it through to the fulfillment.

One night in January, about four years ago, I decided to do something different instead of vegging out in front of the TV. With a notebook and pen, I kicked back in the Lazy Boy and started listing all the things I wanted to do before I died. I was shooting for 50 things, but only ended up with 18. That seemed all right though, because it left plenty of room for new entries along the way.

In the day to day hustle and bustle of life, it is so easy for a person to lose sight or just put off their dreams. There is always something that seems more important. But, if you don't take time for yourself, you too are gonna end up saying, "I wish I had done something like that when I could have."

By writing these dreams down, they become more real, in the sense that they are there in black and white to confront you. There is no escape from how well you're actually doing in wringing what you want out of life.

When you make your list, write down everything you dream about doing, even if some of the things seem way out there. Take into consideration the things your great-grandchildren will admire you for having accomplished.

If out of your list of dreams you only try 10 out of 50, that's OK, because you still will be further ahead than if you didn't go after any. Remember, life is precious and you only go around once.

Scars
Of A Soldier

Vernon Heppe's True Story

By
Gordon Galloway

A Michigan farm boy with an eighth grade education is drafted into the Army during WWII, and becomes a man on the Pacific battlefields of Kwajalein, Leyte and Okinawa. Wounded four times, he received both the Silver and Bronze Star. With a keen sense of humor, Vernon Heppe tells about growing up on the farm and his adjustment to becoming a soldier. He describes combat in vivid detail and the memories that remain.

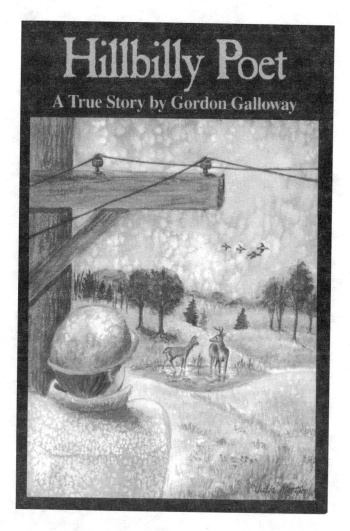

Hillbilly Poet

A True Story by Gordon Galloway

The boy was half Cherokee. He was raised by his blind grandmother until he was sent to an Episcopal boy's home. Ambitious and rebellious, he knew what he wanted out of life, and when the system wouldn't react to his needs, he simply bypassed it.

The mountains and rivers were his refuge and constructing power lines across this country became his vocation. This is a story filled with love, laughter and tears. The last chapter contains Ted Aldridge's poetry. Each peom remembers a special part of his life.

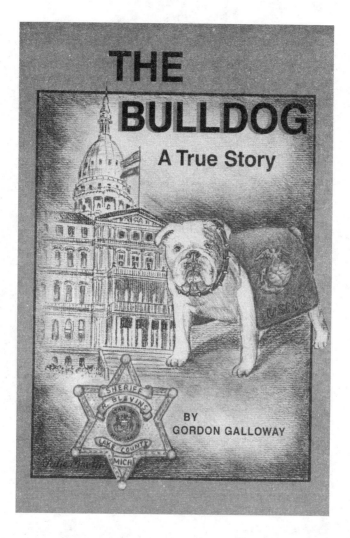

He was half Chippewa and left in a Grand Rapids orphanage. He also
would become one of Michigan's most successful Sheriffs.

This is the true story of a Michigan Sheriff who uncovered corrup-
tion in his county that caused him to be a threat to some of the biggest
names in Michigan politics. Trying to expose this wrongdoing cost
him his career in law enforcement, his reputation, and almost cost him
his life. If you care about the truth, or if you just like a fascinating true
story, you should read THE BULLDOG.

ADDITIONAL COPIES
OF
RIVERS CHANGING
THE BULLDOG
HILLBILLY POET
SCARS OF A SOLDIER

SEND $10 PLUS $1.50 FOR SHIPPING AND HANDLING
(CHECK OR MONEY ORDER)
TO

DEERFIELD PUBLISHING
BOX 146
MORLEY, MI 49336